DIVORCE
in ARIZONA

The Legal Process,
Your Rights, and What to Expect

Second Edition

Marlene A. Pontrelli, Esq.
Robert L. Schwartz, Esq.

Addicus Books
Omaha, Nebraska

An Addicus Nonfiction Book

ISBN: 978-1-943886-71-5

Typography and design by Jack Kusler

The information contained in this publication is of a general nature. Although this book outlines processes and procedures in connection with family law matters in the State of Arizona, it should not be construed nor considered as providing legal advice. Our readers are urged to consult with an attorney of their choice. Every case is different. The facts of each case will determine the particular outcome.

This publication should be used as a general outline of issues and matters to consider in connection with an Arizona family law matters. The authors are not creating by this publication any attorney-client relationship and are not providing specific advice to the reader. We certainly hope that you find the information useful and helpful in navigating your particular circumstances within the State of Arizona.

Library of Congress Cataloging-in-Publication Data

Names: Pontrelli, Marlene A, author. | Schwartz, Robert L. (Lawyer) author.
Title: Divorce in Arizona : the legal process, your rights, and what to expect / Marlene A Pontrelli, Esq., Robert L Schwartz, Esq.
Description: Second edition. | Omaha, Nebraska : Addicus Books, Inc., [2019] | Includes index. | Identifiers: LCCN 2019035121 (print) | LCCN 2019035122 (ebook) | ISBN 9781943886715 (trade paperback) | ISBN 9781950091249 (adobe pdf) | ISBN 9781950091256 (kindle edition) | ISBN 9781950091263 (epub)
Subjects: LCSH: Divorce—Law and legislation—Arizona—Miscellanea.
Classification: LCC KFA2500 .P66 2019 (print) | LCC KFA2500 (ebook) | DDC 346.79101/66—dc23

Addicus Books, Inc.
P.O. Box 45327
Omaha, Nebraska 68145
www.AddicusBooks.com
Printed in the United States of America
10 9 8 7 6 5 4 3 2 1

To our firm Dickinson Wright PLLC.
Without their support and encouragement,
this book would not have been written.

To our clients. Their courage and generosity
of spirit inspire us and teach us daily.

Contents

Acknowledgments

Writing a book that addresses family law issues specific to Arizona has been a long-time goal. When the opportunity to work with Rod Colvin and Jack Kusler of Addicus Books presented itself we were grateful that this goal would finally become a reality. We thank them for their support, encouragement, and guidance. We appreciate their trust in us to participate in their state-specific divorce series of books so that Arizona residents would have an easy to read source of information on frequently asked questions.

Members of our family law group at Dickinson Wright PLLC have contributed more to this book than they realize their depth of knowledge and commitment to excellence have taught and inspired us. Our entire family law team of attorneys, paralegals, and legal assistants is dedicated to making the process of family disputes easier for our clients. We feel honored and privileged to work with such a distinguished group of professionals.

We thank our families and children, who have taught us how important children are in the process and how their unspoken voices must not be ignored. We also thank and acknowledge our clients. Each day they trust us to guide them through a confusing and uncertain time of their lives. They are willing to be courageous, truthful, and vulnerable, reminding us what goes on in the minds and hearts of people experiencing family disputes.

If this book empowers readers on the divorce journey as we hope, it is only because of the generosity of so many, for which we extend our heartfelt gratitude.

Marlene A. Pontrelli, Esq.
Robert L. Schwartz, Esq.
www.dickinsonwright.com

Introduction

Going through a divorce or any family law dispute is one of the most difficult roads to travel. Whether you are the one filing the initial petition or the one responding to the petition, you are facing a change in every single part of your life. No area remains untouched from these issues. Family relationships, friends, children, finances, social networks, personal belongings, a residence, job performance—all affect how your entire personal world is altered in divorce. Our purpose in writing *Divorce in Arizona* is to help you navigate through these uncertain waters.

Divorce and related family law disputes require making tough decisions, which are harder to make without an understanding of the process and procedure. Most people who are facing a divorce have never been to court. The prospect of filing paperwork, responding to paperwork, or going before a judge is often difficult to imagine. *Divorce in Arizona* was written to be a part of helping you move through this time of transition with more clarity and ease. It is not intended to be a substitute for advice from your lawyer and is not providing specific legal advice. Rather, it is designed to assist you in partnering with your lawyer to reach your goals in the resolution of your divorce, and related family law dispute, and to give you information about the process.

In writing *Divorce in Arizona,* we endeavor to explain each step in the hope that it will lead to your empowerment. The more control and clarity you feel over the process, the better you are able to make sound decisions regarding very challenging choices. We hope you will use this book as a guide to ask your lawyer questions; to understand something that may not be clear; and to begin seeing the big picture of the journey upon which you are about to embark.

This book is intended to not only assist you through this process, but also as a guide for professionals who support you— attorneys, mediators, therapists, clergy, financial advisors, and others who are called upon to serve people who are involved in a family law dispute. Although every case is different and your circumstances are unique, we hope that *Divorce in Arizona* will begin to answer your multitude of questions as you begin this brave road toward a new beginning.

Marlene A. Pontrelli, Esq.
Robert L. Schwartz, Esq.

1

Understanding the Divorce Process

At a time when your life can feel like it's in utter chaos, sometimes the smallest bit of predictability can bring a sense of comfort. The outcome of many aspects of your divorce may be unknown, and that certainly increases your fear and anxiety. However, there is one part of your divorce that does have some measure of predictability and that is the divorce process itself. That's where this book is designed to assist you in understanding the process and reducing some of the fear and anxiety about the process.

Going through the divorce process can be a frightening and often intimidating experience. Many people have never had to meet with a lawyer before, or been involved in any type of litigation. At the same time, you are facing the challenges of understanding the legal process, you are also trying to address the emotional issues that often come with the decision to terminate a marriage. The goal of this book is to make you more comfortable with the process and help you make intelligent and informed decisions about your future.

Your lawyer may explain many of the topics in this book in the first consultation. However, you likely will not remember everything that is said during that first meeting. Not only is there is so much information given during the first consultation, but you are often not in the proper emotional state to fully understand everything that is being said. Accordingly, this book will help to refresh some of the things that were discussed with your lawyer and also prompt you to ask questions about items you may not remember.

Most divorces proceed in a step-by-step manner. Despite the uniqueness of your divorce, you can generally count on one phase of your divorce following the next. Sometimes just realizing you are completing stages and moving forward with your divorce reassures you that you are on the correct path.

The first step is to develop a basic understanding of the divorce process. This will lower your anxiety when your attorney starts talking about "depositions" or "going to trial" and you feel your heart start pounding in fear or are anxious about what that actually means. Understanding the steps will also reduce your frustration about the length of the process because you will understand why each step is needed. Each step in the process is like climbing stairs that help you prepare for what comes next. More importantly, understanding the divorce process will make your experience of the entire divorce easier.

1.1 What is my first step?

Find a law firm that handles divorces as a regular part of its law practice. The best recommendations come from people who have knowledge of a lawyer's experience and reputation. Take your time in choosing a lawyer who is right for your case. This is one of the most important decisions you will make with respect to your divorce. Find an attorney you are comfortable discussing your case with as the attorney will likely learn more about your life than is known or shared with even close friends and family. Having a comfort level that this is a person you can speak with freely, who understands your situation, and who will competently represent you is important. The State Bar of Arizona has a list of attorneys who have been certified as specialists in family law if you need to obtain names of potential lawyers in the area of family law.

Even if you are not ready to file for divorce, you may find it helpful to call and schedule an appointment with a lawyer to obtain basic information about protecting yourself and your children. Many times, these initial consultations are to simply explore the process so you know what to expect, especially if you believe your spouse is planning on filing for divorce.

Ask what documents you should bring to your initial consultation. Write down specific questions to ask the attorney. By making a list of your questions to bring to your first meeting you will avoid leaving the office and forgetting to ask one of your questions. In addition to specific questions unique to your circumstances, your questions should include: the attorney's approach to dividing assets, whether your case will involve a claim for spousal support, what you can expect in terms of a timeline, the attorney's form of communication with clients, the amount of retainer required to start the case, and whether the attorney has the time necessary to devote to your case.

Following is a list of questions you may wish to ask your attorney:

- What is your particular experience in family law and in handling this type of situation in particular?
- Do you work evenings and weekends? If something occurs of importance over the weekend, what is your policy for addressing those issues?
- Will you personally be handling my case or will other lawyers or paralegals be assisting?
- What is the best way to communicate with you? (Telephone? E-mail?) How do you charge for each?
- Do you have a policy on how long before you return a telephone call?
- How many times do you expect that we will need to meet in person? Under what circumstances will we need to meet in person?
- What is the specific divorce process and how long do you expect it to take?
- What is the likely cost? (This will be a difficult question for your lawyer to answer. Be wary if you are given a specific cost since so many variables exist, which are unknown at the initial consultation. However, the lawyer may be able to give you an idea of what similar cases have cost, or the potential range of costs depending on whether the action is contested, settled, or litigated.)
- Will there be a need to hire other individuals to assist with the divorce such as financial planners, valuation experts, forensic accountants, or vocational evaluators? If so, what are the likely expenses for these individuals?

3

- If I do not have access to obtain all the financial information, how will the information be obtained?
- Based upon the situation that I have explained, what do you see as the most challenging aspects of my case? How do you believe these challenges should be handled? What is the likely outcome?
- Is this a potential case that may be good for mediation or some other dispute resolution process? Why or why not?
- Are there any steps now that I should take to protect myself financially?
- What are the first steps you would take if I were to retain you?

The lawyer you are considering may not have answers to every question, and rarely can they predict so early in the case what the likely outcome will be. The point of asking the questions, though, is not to necessarily obtain precise answers, but to find out if the lawyer you are consulting with is someone you feel will be able to represent your best interest in a way that is satisfactory to you.

1.2   What steps are taken during the divorce process?

The divorce process in Arizona follows a particular pattern. Following is a list of the steps in the divorce process. The steps are a general overview and are explained in more detail throughout the book.

Obtaining Representation

- Obtain the names of lawyers experienced in family law.
- Schedule an appointment with an attorney for an initial consultation.
- Prepare questions and gather needed documents for initial consultation.
- Meet for initial consultation with attorney.

Make sure you are comfortable with the attorney you are interviewing. If not, take the time to meet with other attorneys, even attorneys within the same firm, until you feel you have the right attorney for your case. This is a journey you will be traveling with your attorney and it is important that there is the right fit for both you and the attorney. Because this is one of the most important aspects of your life and could affect how you live the rest of your life, choose your lawyer carefully to make sure they have the qualifications and time necessary for your case.

- Pay retainer to attorney and sign retainer agreement.
- Provide requested information and documents to your attorney.
- Take other actions as advised by attorney, such as opening or closing financial accounts.

Starting the Process If You Are Filing the Petition

Attorney prepares petition for dissolution of marriage. The petition informs the court of the names of the parties, length of marriage, and if there are any minor children common to the marriage, as well as a basic statement of the issues to be decided and the petitioner's position on the issues.

At the same time the attorney may prepare a motion for temporary orders if temporary orders for such things as temporary support for you or the minor children are needed.

You will review the petition and motion for temporary orders and sign a verification that the facts stated in each are true to the best of your knowledge and belief.

- Attorney files petition with clerk of the court.
- Attorney obtains hearing date for temporary orders if necessary.

The petition is served on your spouse. This can be service by a process server or your spouse may agree to voluntarily accept service by signing and returning an acceptance of service.

Mandatory sixty-day waiting period before a divorce can be finalized begins when a spouse is served or voluntarily accepts service.

Responding to the Petition if Your Spouse Filed First

- Attorney prepares a response to the petition for dissolution of marriage.
- Negotiations begin regarding terms of temporary order on matters such as custody, support, and temporary possession of the family home.

- If there are minor children you must attend a court-approved parenting class within forty-five days.

Preparation of Case

- Gather documents necessary for your case, which may include obtaining documents from third parties such as financial institutions.
- Prepare an *affidavit of financial information* that lists income and expenses.
- Prepare a list of property and debts.

Disclosures statements under Rule 49 of the Arizona Rules of Family Law Procedure must be prepared and submitted to the other side within forty days or as set by the court.

Resolution Management Conference

This is generally the first time the parties are in court. The parties and their attorneys attend a brief meeting with the judge to discuss potential issues and whether there is any resolution to the issues. If there's no resolution, the judge will set a date for temporary orders, if necessary, and a trial date.

- Temporary hearing held if no resolution on a temporary basis.
- Both sides conduct *discovery* to obtain information regarding all relevant facts. Obtain valuations of all assets, including expert opinions if needed.
- Confer with attorney to review facts, identify issues, assess strengths and weaknesses of case, review strategy, and develop proposal for settlement.
- Spouses, with support of attorneys, attempt to reach agreement through written proposals, mediation, settlement conferences, or other negotiation.
- Parties reach agreement on all issues.

Attorney prepares decree, property settlement agreement, and if there are minor children, a parenting plan. If there are retirement plans such as a 401(k) or a pension, a *qualified domestic relations order* needs to be prepared to divide the retirement funds so it is non-taxable event.

In the event of no settlement

- A certificate of readiness and memorandum to set trial is filed if the court has not already set a court date.

- Parties prepare for trial on unresolved issues.

Trial preparations proceed including preparation of witnesses, trial exhibits, legal research on contested issues, pretrial motions, trial brief, preparation of direct and cross-examination of witnesses, preparation of opening statement, subpoena of witnesses, closing argument, and suggestions to the court.

- Meet with attorney for final trial preparation.
- Trial is held.
- The judge takes the matter under advisement.
- The judge will issue a decree of dissolution in approximately thirty to sixty days.
- Documents required to divide retirement accounts and ensure the payment of spousal and child support submitted to the court.
- Attorney will prepare closing letter.

1.3 Must I have an attorney to get a divorce in Arizona?

You are not required to have an attorney to obtain a divorce in Arizona. However, if your case involves children, spousal maintenance, significant property, or debts, you may find it easier to have an attorney than proceeding on your own.

If your divorce does not involve any of these issues, contact the self-help center at the superior court in your county or call the clerk of the court to request documents and instructions that may be used in filing your own case and proceeding on your own. In some counties, the forms are available online. A listing of available resources with applicable websites and telephone numbers is included the Resources section in the back of the book. A person who proceeds in a legal matter without a lawyer is referred to as being in *pro per* or *pro se,* on one's own.

If you are considering proceeding without an attorney, you may want to at least have an initial consultation with an attorney to discuss your rights and duties under the law. You may have certain rights or obligations you are unaware of. Meeting with a lawyer can help you decide whether to proceed on your own.

1.4 Is Arizona a *no-fault* state or do I need grounds for a divorce?

Arizona is a *no-fault* divorce state. This means that neither spouse is required to prove that the other is "at fault" in order to be granted a divorce. Factors such as infidelity, cruelty, or abandonment are not necessary to receive a divorce in Arizona. The only ground for the divorce is that the marriage is "irretrievably broken."

This ground is stated in the initial petition. If you are responding to the *petition for dissolution of marriage* and also believe the marriage is irretrievably broken, you can simply agree in your response.

1.5 What if my spouse alleges that the marriage is irretrievably broken but I do not think that it is?

The petition for dissolution will likely allege just a general ground for the divorce that the marriage is irretrievably broken. So, what can you do if you believe there is hope for reconciliation?

You can dispute that the marriage is irretrievably broken by denying the allegation in your response to the petition. In such circumstances, the court will then take evidence on this issue at the final hearing. However, it is virtually impossible to show that the marriage is not irretrievably broken unless both parties agree. However, talk to your lawyer about the possibility of filing a *petition for referral to conciliation services*.

If you are responding to the petition for dissolution and believe that there is a basis for reconciliation, you can file a petition for a referral to conciliation services. Conciliation services are available in some courts as a means to put the divorce action on hold until there is an opportunity to meet with a court representative and determine whether there is the ability to repair the marriage. For example, if the reason the parties are divorcing is due to disputes over financial issues, it may be that putting in place a financial plan and having both parties agree to the financial plan will avoid the necessity of obtaining a divorce. If a petition for conciliation services has been filed, no action can be taken with respect to the divorce until a notice is obtained from conciliation services that conciliation efforts have failed.

8

If the conciliation efforts fail and testimony regarding whether the marriage is irretrievably broken is required, all that is needed is testimony from one party stating that efforts at reconciliation were made, that those efforts were not successful, that further attempts would not be beneficial, and that the marriage is therefore irretrievably broken.

The judge may ask for information regarding the nature of the problems that led to the divorce or the types of reconciliation efforts made, such as using conciliation services or counseling with a therapist or clergy member.

There is one caveat unique to couples married in Arizona with respect to "no-fault" divorces. If the parties have a "covenant" marriage, certain other requirements must be met. A *covenant marriage* is one where the parties agree that they are committed to each other and will take all reasonable efforts to preserve the marriage and be bound by the law in Arizona related to covenant marriages. The parties can declare this desire to enter into a covenant marriage on the application for a marriage license. A husband and wife may also, after marriage, convert the existing marriage to a covenant marriage. If your marriage is a covenant marriage, the basis and timing for obtaining a legal separation or a divorce are limited. If you have a covenant marriage, speak to your attorney about the grounds and timing for terminating your marriage.

1.6 How will a judge view infidelity or my spouse's infidelity?

Because Arizona is a no-fault divorce state, there will rarely be testimony or evidence introduced about either spouse's infidelity. However, this testimony may still come in if community funds were used to pay for such things as dinners, hotels, airfares, or gifts because the expenditure of those funds on an extramarital affair would be considered expenditures for a non-community purpose. In such cases, a claim can be made for reimbursement of one-half of the funds that were spent.

1.7 Do I have to get divorced in the same state I was married in?

No. Regardless of where you were married, you may seek a divorce in Arizona if the jurisdictional requirements of residency are met and the marriage is not considered void in Arizona. The law that will be applied is Arizona law, not the law of the place you were married.

1.8 How long must I have lived in Arizona to get a divorce in the state?

Either you or your spouse must have been domiciled (where you intend to permanently reside) in Arizona for at least ninety days prior to the filing of a petition for dissolution of marriage to meet the residency requirement for a divorce in Arizona.

If neither party meets the residency requirement, other legal options are still available for your protection. If you do not meet the ninety-day residency requirement, talk to your attorney about options such as a legal separation, a petition for legal decision-making and parenting time if there are minor children, or an order of protection.

1.9. What is a *void* marriage?

Arizona will not grant a divorce if the marriage is not recognized as a valid marriage in Arizona. A void marriage in Arizona is one between certain members of a family, such as between brothers and sisters, grandparents and grandchildren, aunts and uncles, and first cousins.

1.10 My spouse has told me he or she will never "give" me a divorce. Can I get one in Arizona anyway?

Yes. Arizona does not require that your spouse agree to a divorce. If your spouse threatens to not "give" you a divorce, know that in Arizona this is likely to be an idle threat without any basis in the law.

Under Arizona law, to obtain a divorce you must be able to prove that your marriage is "irretrievably broken." This is a legal term meaning that one sees no possibility of reconciliation between you or your spouse. In short, it is not necessary to have your spouse agree to the divorce or to allege the specific difficulties that arose during the marriage to obtain a divorce in Arizona, just that at least one party can state that the marriage is irretrievably broken.

1.11 Can I divorce my spouse in Arizona if he or she lives in another state?

Provided you have met the residency requirements for living in Arizona for ninety days, you can file for divorce here even if your spouse lives in another state.

Discuss with your attorney the facts that will need to be proven and the steps necessary to give your spouse proper notice to ensure that the court will have jurisdiction (that is the power to decide your case) over your spouse. Your attorney can counsel you on whether it is possible to proceed with the divorce.

1.12 Can I get a divorce even when I don't know where my spouse is currently living?

Arizona law allows you to proceed with a divorce even if you do not know the current address of your spouse. First, take action to attempt to locate your spouse. Contact family members, friends, former coworkers, or anyone else who might know your spouse's whereabouts. Utilize resources on the Internet that are designed to help locate people. You may even consider hiring an investigator.

Let your attorney know of the efforts you have made to attempt to find your spouse. Inform your lawyer of your spouse's last known address, as well as any work address or other address where this person may be found. After your attorney attempts to give notice to your spouse without success, it is possible to ask the court to proceed with the divorce by giving notice through publication in a newspaper.

Although your divorce may be granted following service of notice by publication in a newspaper, you may not be able to get other court orders such as those for spousal support or child support without giving personal notice to your spouse. Talk to your attorney about your options and rights if you don't know where your spouse is living.

1.13 I just moved to a different county within the state of Arizona. Do I have to file in the county where my spouse lives?

You may file your divorce complaint either in the county where you are domiciled (where you permanently reside) or in the county where your spouse is domiciled (permanently resides).

1.14 I immigrated to Arizona. Will my immigration status stop me from getting a divorce?

If you meet the residency requirements for divorce in Arizona you can get a divorce here notwithstanding your immigration status. Talk to your immigration lawyer about the likelihood of a divorce leading to immigration challenges.

If you are a victim of domestic violence, tell your lawyer. You may be eligible for a change in your immigration status under the federal *Violence Against Women Act.*

1.15 I want to get divorced in my Indian tribal court. What do I need to know?

Each tribal court has its own laws governing divorce. Requirements for residency, grounds for divorce, and the laws regarding property, support, and children can vary substantially from state law. Some tribes have very different laws governing the grounds for your divorce, removal of children from the home, and cohabitation.

Contact an attorney who is knowledgeable about the law in your tribal court for legal advice on pursuing a divorce in your tribal court or on the requirements for recording a divorce obtained in state court with the clerk of the tribal court.

1.16 Is there a waiting period for a divorce in Arizona?

Yes. Arizona has a mandatory sixty-day waiting period. This waiting period begins on the day that the respondent, the person who did not initiate the divorce process, is determined to have been given legal notice of the divorce. This date is either the day that the respondent is personally delivered papers by an authorized process server or the date that the respondent files with the court a voluntary acceptance of service acknowledging that he or she knows the divorce has been filed with the court and accepting the papers that initiate the divorce process.

1.17   What is a *petition for dissolution of marriage?*

A *petition for dissolution of marriage* is a document signed by the person filing for divorce and filed with the clerk of the court to start the divorce process. The petition will set forth in very general terms what the petitioner is asking the court to order. For example, some of the statements in the petition may include the following:

For the petition for dissolution of marriage (with minor child), petitioner alleges that:

- Petitioner and respondent, has been domiciled in the county of Maricopa, State of Arizona, for a period of at least ninety (90) days prior to the filing of this petition. The state of Arizona has been the marital domicile of the petitioner and respondent.
- The parties do not have a covenant marriage.
- The conciliation provisions of A.R.S. §25-381.09 and §25-351 et. seq. either do not apply or have been met.
- The parties' marriage is irretrievably broken and there is no reasonable prospect of reconciliation.
- The parties have one (1) minor child in common.
- Petitioner believes that both parties should make decisions in the best interest of the parties' child Therefore, the court should order the parties to exercise joint legal decision-making of the parties' minor child. Petitioner should be awarded primary physical custody of the minor children, with reasonable parenting time by respondent in accordance with the best interest of the minor child.
- Child support should be ordered in accordance with the Arizona Child Support Guidelines and A.R.S. §25-320.
- The parties, during their marriage, have acquired certain assets, including joint, common, and community property, and have incurred certain joint and community debts and liabilities that should be equitably divided between them.
- The parties have not reached any agreements regarding custody, parenting time, child support, spousal maintenance, or the division of property and debts.

13

- Based upon the factors set forth in A.R.S. §25-319(A), including the property to be attributed to each spouse, the earning ability of each spouse in the labor market, the contribution to the opportunities of the other spouse, and the length of the marriage, neither party is entitled to an award of spousal maintenance.

1.18 My spouse said he or she filed for divorce last week, but my lawyer says there's nothing on file at the courthouse. What does it mean to "file for divorce"?

When lawyers use the term "filing" they are usually referring to filing a legal document at the courthouse, such as delivering the petition for dissolution of marriage to the clerk of the court. Sometimes a person who has hired a lawyer to begin a divorce action uses the phrase "I've filed for divorce," although no papers have yet been taken to the courthouse to start the legal process.

1.19 If we both want a divorce, does it matter who files?

No. In the eyes of the court, the *petitioner* (the party who files the complaint initiating the divorce process) and the *respondent* (the other spouse) are not seen differently by virtue of which party filed. The court, as a neutral decision-maker, will not give preference to either party. Both parties will be given adequate notice and each will have a chance to be heard and present arguments. The only difference is that if the matter proceeds to trial, the petitioner presents their case first, and then the respondent presents second.

1.20 Are there advantages to filing first?

It depends. Discuss with your attorney whether there are any advantages to you filing first. Your attorney may advise you to file first or to wait until your spouse files, depending upon the overall strategy for your case and your circumstances. For example, if there is a concern that your spouse will begin transferring assets upon learning about your plans for divorce, your attorney might advise you to file and have the papers served first so that the *preliminary injunction* immediately goes into effect to prove such action. Along with a petition for dissolution a preliminary injunction is served on the responding party advising that no assets are to be transferred and no community assets disposed of except in specific circumstances. Unauthorized transfers that occur will then constitute a violation of the preliminary injunction and your spouse will be held liable to you for damages resulting from such violation. Your attorney may also advise seeking a temporary restraining order to protect against such an action. However, if you are separated from your spouse but have a beneficial temporary arrangement, your attorney may counsel you to wait for your spouse to file.

1.21 Is the filing or granting of my divorce a matter of public record?

Documents filed with the court, such as the petition for dissolution or a final decree, are matters of public record. Generally, the docket of each case is available online and is searchable by first and last name or case number. However, unless the county in which you live provides online access to court rulings, someone requesting to see the actual court papers would have to go down to the courthouse and request access to the file.

In rare cases, a divorce file may be kept private, referred to as being *sealed* or *under seal* if the court orders it. Discuss with your attorney whether at least portions of your case may be "sealed." All confidential information, such as home addresses, birthdates, and Social Security numbers, are filed on a sensitive data sheet which is not part of the public record.

1.22 Is there a way to avoid embarrassing my spouse and not have a process server give the divorce papers to him or her at their workplace?

Talk to your lawyer about the option of having your spouse sign a document known as an acceptance of service. The signing and filing of this document with the court can eliminate the need to have your spouse served with papers.

15

Sample Letter to Spouse

Dear _____:

I am counsel for the Petitioner in the above matter, which was filed on _____, 20__. Rather than have you personally served, we are enclosing the following documents:

1. Summons;

2. Petition for Dissolution of Non-Covenant Marriage (With Minor Children);

3. Preliminary Injunction;

4. Notice Regarding Creditors;

5. Notice Regarding Health Insurance;

6. Order and Notice to Attend Parent Information Program Class; and

7. Acceptance of Service

If you have already or plan to retain an attorney, please provide the enclosed documents to that individual and have him or her contact me at their convenience.

If you will accept service of the above documents, please sign the enclosed Acceptance of Service, have your signature notarized, and return it to my office. If I do not receive the Acceptance of Service back from you within a few days, the Petitioner will need to incur the expense of a process server to serve you with the documents. The Acceptance of Service merely acknowledges that you received the above documents. By signing the Acceptance of Service, you are not stating that you agree with the documents, only that you have received the documents.

Thank you for your anticipated cooperation.

Sample Acceptance of Service

In re the Marriage of:

Case No. _____

ACCEPTANCE OF SERVICE

_____,

Petitioner,

and

_____,

Respondent.

1.   My name is _____, and I am the Respondent named above and I agree to voluntarily accept service process pursuant to ARFLP 40(F).

2   I have received a copy of the Summons, Petition for Dissolution of Marriage, Notice Regarding Creditors, Notice Regarding Health Insurance, Order and Notice to Attend Parent Information Program Class that have been filed and issued in this action, and agree that this action may proceed against me as though I had been personally served within the State of Arizona.

I have read the foregoing document and know of my own knowledge that the facts stated herein are true and correct.

_____

(Name of Respondent)

STATE OF ARIZONA	)
	) ss.
County of Maricopa	)

This instrument was acknowledged before me this _____ day of _____, 20__, by the person above subscribed; and if subscribed in a representative capacity, then for the principal named and in the capacity indicated; and this person or persons subscribed and swore to the same before me.

IN WITNESS THEREOF, I hereunder set my hand and official seal.

_____

NOTARY PUBLIC
My Commission Expires:_____

The use of an acceptance of service is not appropriate for all cases, so discuss with your attorney the best choice for your case.

- What you would like the judge to order in your case.
- Remain respectful toward your spouse throughout the process.
- Keep your children out of the litigation.
- Comply with any temporary court orders, such as support orders.
- Advise your attorney of any significant developments in your case.

By doing your part in the divorce process, you enable your attorney to partner with you for a better outcome while also lowering your attorney fees.

1.23 Should I sign an acceptance of service even if I don't agree with what my spouse has written in the complaint for divorce?

Signing the acceptance of service does not mean that you agree with anything your spouse has stated in the petition for dissolution or anything that your spouse is asking for in the divorce.

Signing the acceptance of service only substitutes for having a process server personally hand you the documents. You do not waive the right to object to anything your spouse has stated in the petition for dissolution of marriage.

Follow your attorney's advice on whether and when to sign an acceptance of service. Because the community of assets that you accumulate jointly ceases on the date you accept service of the petition for dissolution of marriage, there may be timing considerations that you will want to discuss with your lawyer. In addition, your time to respond to the petition begins when you accept service so it is important to calendar this date and make sure that you respond in a timely manner. In most cases, if you already have retained a lawyer, the lawyer will accept service on your behalf.

1.24 Why should I contact an attorney right away if I have received divorce papers?

If your spouse has filed for divorce, it is important that you obtain legal advice as soon as possible. Even if you and your spouse are getting along, having independent legal counsel can help you make decisions now that could affect your divorce later. In addition, you will need to file a response within twenty days after you have been served with papers. Accordingly, to avoid being in default and not responding in a timely manner, your lawyer will need to know the date you have been served and file a timely response or obtain an extension to file a response.

1.25 In addition to the petition for dissolution, there are many other documents I have been given. What are these documents?

In addition to the petition for dissolution, a number of other documents are filed to start your proceedings. The documents have important information that you should be aware of:

- *Summons.* This is the document that advises the respondent that he or she has twenty days to respond to the petition after service. A failure to respond to the petition allows the petitioner to take a default judgment.

- *Preliminary Injunction.* The preliminary injunction forbids certain actions during the pendency of the matter until the judge signs a decree or further court order. This includes selling community property and taking a minor child out of Arizona without a written agreement from your spouse.

- *Order to Attend Parent Information Class.* Every parent must take a four-hour parenting class. You can do the class in person or sometimes online classes are also available. The class must be completed within forty-five days. Approved parenting classes are listed on the notice that you will receive. Discuss with your attorney the possibility of taking the class online or if you are in another state a class in your state that will satisfy the Arizona requirement.

19

- *Notice Regarding Creditors.* This document is used if a party wants to obtain account information from creditors. Discuss with your attorney whether this information is needed.
- *Notice Regarding Your Rights about Health Insurance Coverage.* This document advises that when the divorce is final, each party is responsible for obtaining their own health insurance.

1.26   What is a *resolution management conference?*

Some courts will hold as the initial proceeding in the matter a resolution management conference. A resolution management conference is an opportunity for the attorneys and parties to appear before the court and advise the court of the nature of the matter. This allows the judge to learn the length of the marriage, whether there are minor children involved, what issues are likely to be in dispute, and how long it will take the parties to prepare for trial. This is also an opportunity for the parties to advise the court of any agreements they have reached that do not need to be addressed by the court, such as an agreement as to parenting time for the minor children, division of assets, or payment of support.

1.27   What is a *temporary orders hearing?*

Anytime a petition for dissolution of marriage or legal separation has been filed, a temporary orders hearing may be scheduled. This hearing is scheduled when one party has filed a motion for temporary orders.

A *temporary orders hearing* is a short proceeding (generally no more than one or two hours). At the hearing the court addresses specific issues that need to be resolved on a temporary basis, such a payment of community expenses, payment of support, and parenting time. The orders are only temporary and may be changed at any time during the course of the proceedings, or at the time of a final decree.

The purpose is simply a way for the court to have some orders in place before a final hearing is held so that community expenses do not go unpaid, or one party is not left without any way to pay for basic necessities. In addition, if there are children, it is important to have a temporary parenting time schedule. Because temporary orders are usually done at the beginning of a case it is possible you will receive only a few days' notice of a temporary orders hearing. Your lawyer will discuss with you preparation for the temporary orders hearing.

1.28 After my petition for divorce is filed, how soon can a temporary hearing be held to decide what happens with our child and our finances while the divorce is pending?

In most cases a temporary orders hearing can be held within forty-five days of your divorce being filed with the court. The court will generally set a brief return hearing within ten to fifteen days after the filing of the motion for temporary orders in order to see what issues can be resolved without a hearing. The parties and their lawyers are required to meet in advance of the return hearing to try and settle temporary orders. Temporary orders are without prejudice to assert a different position at the time of the final hearing, and the court is not bound to follow the temporary orders at the final hearing. Rather temporary orders are simply that—temporary. It is a way to help move the case along and provide some orders to be followed during the pendency of the action.

1.29 During my divorce, what am I responsible for doing?

Your attorney will explain what actions you should take to further the divorce process and to help you reach the best possible outcome.

You will be asked to:

- Keep in regular contact with your attorney.
- Update your attorney regarding any changes in your contact information, such as address, phone numbers, and e-mail address.
- Provide your attorney with all requested documents.
- Provide requested information in a timely manner.
- Complete forms and questionnaires.
- Appear in court on time.
- Be direct about asking any questions you might have.
- Tell your attorney your thoughts on settlement or what you would like the judge to order in your case.

- Remain respectful toward your spouse throughout the process.
- Keep your children out of the litigation.
- Comply with any temporary court orders, such as support orders.
- Advise your attorney of any significant developments in your case.

By doing your part in the divorce process, you enable your attorney to partner with you for a better outcome while also lowering your attorney fees.

1.30 I'm worried that I won't remember to ask my lawyer about all of the issues in my case. How can I be sure I don't miss anything?

Write down all of the topics you want to discuss with your attorney, including what your goals are for the outcome of the divorce. The sooner you clarify your goals, the easier it will be for your attorney to support you to help you each reach those goals. Realize that your attorney will think of some issues that you may not be thinking of. Your lawyer's experience will be helpful in making sure nothing important is not forgotten.

Divorce Issues Checklist

Issue	Notes
Dissolution of marriage	
Parenting time for minor children	
Removal of children from Arizona	
Parenting plan	
Child support	
Deviation from child-support guidelines	
Termination of child support	
Travel expenses to facilitate parenting time for out-of-town/state parents	
Life insurance to fund unpaid child support	
Automatic witholding for support	
Payment of child support arrearages	

Divorce Issues Checklist (Continued)

Issue	Notes
Child-care expenses	
Child-care credit	
Health insurance for minor children	
Uninsured medical expenses for minor children	
Payment of extracurricular activities for minor children	
Private school tuition for children	
College expenses for children	
College savings accounts for the benefit of children	
Health insurance on the parties	
Real property: marital residence	
Real property: rentals, cabins, commercial property, etc.	
Time-shares	
Retirement accounts	
Federal or military pensions	
Business interests	
Bank accounts	
Investments	
Stock options	
Stock purchase plans	
Life insurance policies	
Frequent flyer miles	
Credit card points	
Season tickets for events	
Premarital or noncommunity assets	
Premarital or noncommunity debts	

Divorce Issues Checklist (Continued)

Issue	Notes
Pets	
Personal property division: including motor vehicles, recreational vehicles, campers, airplanes, collections, furniture, electronics, tools, household goods	
Exchange date for personal property	
Division of community debt	
Property settlement	
Spousal support	
Life insurance to fund unpaid spousal support	
Arrearage of spousal support from temporary order	
Tax exemption for minor children	
IRS Form 8332	
Filing status for tax returns for last/current year	
Former name restoration	
Attorney's fees	

1.31 My spouse has all of our financial information. How will I be able to prepare for negotiations and trial if I don't know the facts or have the documents?

After your divorce has been filed with the court and temporary matters have been addressed, your attorney will proceed with a process known as *discovery*.

Through discovery, your attorney can ask your spouse to provide documents and information needed to prepare your case. Your attorney can also subpoena information directly from all financial institutions where accounts are held to obtain the requested documentation.

Some information is required under Rule 49 of the Arizona Rules of Family Law Procedure to be voluntarily exchanged between the parties. Ask your attorney for the categories of documents required to be exchanged under Rule 49.

1.32 My spouse and I both want our divorce to be amicable. How can we keep it that way?

You and your spouse are to be acknowledged for your willingness to cooperate while focusing on moving through the divorce process. This will not only make your lives easier and save you money on attorney fees, but it is also more likely to result in an outcome you are both satisfied with.

Find a lawyer who understands your goal to reach settlement and encourage your spouse to do the same. Cooperate with the prompt exchange of necessary information. Then ask your attorney about the options of mediation and negotiation for reaching agreement. Even if you are not able to settle all of the issues in your divorce, these actions can increase the likelihood of agreement on many of the terms of your divorce decree.

1.33 Can I choose my judge?

You may not choose your own judge or judge "shop." "Judge shopping" occurs when a person involved in a legal case attempts to influence the court's assignment of a case so that it will be directed to or away from a particular judge.

However, talk to your attorney about the reasons you want a different judge. If you believe that your judge has a conflict of interest, such as being a close friend of your spouse, you may have a basis for asking the judge to be "recused" in order to allow another judge to hear the case. In addition, every party is allowed to file for a change of judge one time. Accordingly, if there is a reason you may not want a particular judge and have not filed a notice to change judges previously, you will be permitted to change to a different judge. You do not have a choice of who the new assigned judge will be.

1.34 How long will it take to get my divorce?

The more you and your spouse are in agreement, the faster your divorce will conclude. At a minimum, there will be a sixty-day wait from the date of service of the petition for dissolution on the spouse who did not file for divorce or from the date the non-filing spouse filed an acceptance of service with the court.

Assuming all issues, such as parenting time, support, property, and debts, are completely settled between you and your spouse, a consent decree can be submitted to the judge for his or her approval after the sixty-day waiting period. After being signed by the judge, your divorce will be final.

1.35   What is the significance of my divorce being final?

The finality of your divorce decree, sometimes referred to as the *decree of dissolution of marriage,* is important for many reasons. It affects your right to remarry, your eligibility for health insurance from your former spouse, and filing status for income taxes.

1.36   When does my divorce become final?

The date that triggers the time period for a divorce becoming final is the date that the divorce decree is entered and filed by the clerk of the court.

1.37   Can I start using my former name right away and how do I get my name legally restored?

Your divorce decree will indicate whether you wish to be restored to a former name (or even if you wish to pick a new name). After the decree is signed indicating restoration of your former name, or new name, you may begin using your changed name. Many agencies and institutions, however, will not alter their records without a certified copy of the decree indicating your new name. Ask your lawyer to obtain certified copies of the decree for you so you can submit the decree to the appropriate agencies and institutions.

If you want to change your legal name after the divorce and have not provided for it in your decree, it will be necessary for you to undergo a separate legal action for a name change.

2

Coping with Stress during the Divorce Process

It may have been a few years ago. Or it may have been many years ago. Perhaps it was only months. But when you said, "I do," you meant it. Like most people getting married, you planned to be a happily married couple for life.

But things happen. Life brings change. People change. Whatever the circumstance, you now find yourself considering divorce. The emotions of divorce run from one extreme to another as you journey through the process. You may feel relief and ready to move on with your life. On the other hand, you may feel emotions that are quite painful. Anger. Fear. Sorrow. A deep sense of loss. Failure. Remember, it is important to find support for coping with all these strong emotions.

Because going through a divorce can be an emotional time, having a clear understanding of the divorce process and what to expect will help you make better decisions. And when it comes to decision-making, search inside yourself to clarify your intentions and goals for the future. Let these intentions be your guide.

2.1 My spouse left home weeks ago. I don't want a divorce because I feel our marriage can be saved. Should I still see an attorney?

Yes, it is still a good idea to see an attorney even if you think your marriage can be saved. Whether you want a divorce or not, there may be important actions for you to take now to protect your assets, credit, home, children, and future right to support. If your spouse files for divorce, a temporary hearing could be heard in just a matter of days. It is best to be prepared with the support of an attorney, even if you want to try and resolve the differences with your spouse.

Your lawyer can also advise you about how to file a petition for conciliation services. The purpose of filing for conciliation services is to attempt to preserve the marriage by amicably settling any controversies between the parties. The judge of the conciliation court will set a time and place for the hearing to determine whether an amicable resolution can be reached. The hearing is informal and may be one conference or a series of conferences to effect a reconciliation. The petition for conciliation services can be filed prior to any dissolution action being filed, or even after your spouse has filed for divorce. No steps toward obtaining a divorce or legal separation can take place until the presiding officer conducting the conferences determines that there is no likelihood that there will be a reconciliation and terminates the proceedings. At that point the proceedings will then continue in the superior court.

2.2   The thought of going to a lawyer's office to talk about divorce is more than I can bear. I canceled the first appointment I made because I just couldn't do it. What should I do?

Sometimes the most difficult part of the process is making that first call to set an appointment with the lawyer. Many people going through a divorce never have had to speak with a lawyer and this is the first time. It is natural for you to feel anxious about the experience. Your lawyer understands this and will try to make you feel as relaxed as possible. You may want to ask a trusted friend or family member to go with you to the appointment. Even if they do not sit in on the consultation, having someone in the waiting area to support you will help you feel less nervous about the experience. After you meet with your lawyer, it is very likely that you will feel greatly relieved just to be better informed.

2.3 **There is some information about my marriage that I think my attorney needs, but I'm too embarrassed to discuss it. Must I tell the attorney?**

Your attorney has an ethical duty to maintain confidentiality. Past events in your marriage are matters that your lawyer is obligated to keep private. Attorneys who practice divorce law are accustomed to hearing a lot of intimate information about families. Although it is deeply personal to you, it is unlikely that anything you tell your lawyer will be a shock.

It may feel uncomfortable for a short moment, but it is important that your attorney have complete information so that your interests can be fully protected. If speaking directly about these facts still seems too hard, consider putting them in a letter.

2.4 **I'm unsure about how to tell our children about the divorce, and I'm worried I'll say the wrong thing. What's the best way?**

How you talk to your children about the divorce will depend upon their ages and development. Changes in your children's everyday lives, such as a change of residence or one parent leaving the home, are far more important to them. Information about legal proceedings and meetings with lawyers are best kept among adults.

Simpler answers are best for young children. Avoid giving them more information than they need. Sometimes it is best to not mention the word "divorce" to them. Instead, explain that mommy and daddy have decided it is better for them to be friends than to continue to live in the same house together.

After the initial discussion, keep the door open to further talks by creating opportunities for them to talk about the situation. Use these times to acknowledge their feelings and offer support. Always assure them that none of this is their fault and that they are still loved by both you and your spouse, regardless of the fact that you will not all be living together. A Child's Perspective on Divorce is included in the Appendix.

2.5   My youngest child seems very depressed about the divorce, the middle one is angry, and my teenager is skipping school. How can I cope?

A child's reaction to divorce can vary depending upon his or her age and other factors. Some may cry and beg for reconciliation, and others may behave inappropriately. Reducing conflict with your spouse, being a consistent and nurturing parent, and making sure both of you remain involved are all actions that can support your children regardless of how they are reacting to the divorce.

Support groups for children whose parents are divorcing are also available at many schools and religious communities. A school counselor can also provide support. If more help is needed, confer with a therapist experienced in working with children.

2.6   I am so frustrated by my spouse's "Disneyland parent" behavior. Is there anything I can do to stop this?

Feelings of guilt, competition, or remorse sometimes lead a parent to be tempted to spend parenting time in trips to the toy store and special activities. Other times these feelings can result in an absence of discipline in an effort to become the favored parent or to make the time "special."

Shift your focus from the other parent's behavior to your own, and do your best to be an outstanding parent during this time. This includes keeping a routine for your child for family meals, bedtimes, chores, and homework. Encourage family activities, as well as individual time with each child, when it's possible.

During the time when a child's life is changing, providing a consistent and stable routine in your home can ease his or her anxiety and provide comfort. If you are sharing parenting time in different homes, consider how you refer to the other parent's home. It should not be you are going to dad's house or mom's house. That makes the child feel as if neither house is their house. Instead refer to it by the city if you reside in different cities, or by street name, (for example, the Central Avenue house and the Broadway Blvd. house). That makes the child feel like they have two homes versus no home that is theirs.

2.7   Between requests for information from my spouse's lawyer and my own lawyer, I am totally overwhelmed. How do I manage gathering all of this detailed information by the deadlines imposed?

First, simply get started. Often the thought about a task is worse than the job itself.

Second, break it down into smaller tasks. Perhaps one evening you gather your tax returns, and on the weekend, you work on your monthly living expenses.

Third, let in support. Ask that friend of yours who just loves numbers to come over for an evening with her calculator to help you get organized.

Finally, communicate with your lawyer. Your attorney or paralegal may be able to make your job easier by giving you suggestions or help. It may be that essential information can be provided now and the details submitted later.

2.8   I am so depressed about my divorce that I'm having difficulty getting out of bed in the morning to care for my children. What should I do?

See your health care provider. Feelings of depression are common during a divorce. You also want to make sure that you identify any physical health concerns.

Although feelings of sadness are common during a divorce, more serious depression means it's time to seek professional support.

Your health and your ability to care for your children are both essential. Follow through on recommendations by your health care professionals for therapy, medication, or other measures to improve your wellness. Share your health concerns with your lawyer as well so that your case can be managed in a way that does not cause you unnecessary stress.

2.9   Will taking prescribed medication to help treat my insomnia and depression hurt my case?

Not necessarily. Talk to your health care professional and follow their recommendations. Taking care of your health is of the utmost importance during this difficult time, and will serve your best interest as well as the best interest of your children. Inform your attorney of any medications that you are taking or treatment that you are seeking. It is not the taking of medication that usually hurts your case; rather, it is the failure to: recognize the issues, follow a prescribed regimen, and get the emotional help and treatment that is needed. These factors help determine whether you can be the very best parent for your children.

2.10 I know I need help to cope with the stress of the divorce, but I can't afford counseling. What can I do?

You are wise to recognize that divorce is a time for seeking support. You can explore a number of options, including:

- Meeting with a member of the clergy or lay chaplain
- Joining a divorce support group
- Turning to friends and family members
- Going to a therapist or divorce coach. If budget is a concern, contact a social agency that offers counseling services on a sliding fee scale.

Additionally, there are several resources included at the back of this book that should be consulted to help determine if free counseling is available to you. If none of these options are available, look again at your budget. You may see that counseling is important enough that you decide to find a way to increase your income or lower your expenses to support this investment in your well-being.

2.11 I'm the one who filed for divorce, but I still have loving feelings toward my spouse and feel sad about divorcing. Does this mean I should dismiss my divorce?

Strong feelings of caring about your spouse often persist after a divorce is filed. Whether to proceed with a divorce is a deeply personal decision. Although feelings can inform us of our thoughts, sometimes they can also cause us to not look at everything there is to see in our situation.

Have you and your spouse participated in marriage counseling? Has your spouse refused to seek treatment for an addiction? Are you worried about the safety of you or your children if you remain in the marriage? Can you envision yourself as financially secure if you remain in this marriage? Is your spouse involved in another relationship?

The answers to these questions can help you clarify whether to consider reconciliation. Talk to your therapist, coach, or spiritual advisor to help determine the right path for you.

2.12 Will my lawyer charge me for the time I spend talking about my feelings about my spouse and my divorce?
It depends. If you are paying your attorney by the hour, expect to be charged for the time your attorney spends talking with you. If your attorney is being paid a flat rate for handling your divorce, the time spent talking with you will be included in the fee.

2.13 My lawyer doesn't seem to realize how difficult my divorce is for me. How can I get him to understand?
Everyone wants support and compassion from the professionals who help during a divorce. Speak frankly with your attorney about your concerns. It may be that your lawyer does not see your concerns as being relevant to the job of getting your desired outcome in the divorce. Your willingness to improve the communication will help your lawyer understand how best to support you in the process and will help you understand which matters are best left for discussion with your therapist or a supportive friend.

2.14 I've been told not to speak ill of my spouse in front of my child, but I know my spouse is doing this all the time. Why can't I just speak the truth?
It can be devastating for your child to hear you bad-mouthing his or her other parent. What your child needs is permission to love both of you, regardless of any bad parental behavior. The best way to support your child during this time is to encourage a positive relationship with the other parent. In the Appendix is a list of ten things your child would say if they could really tell you what they are thinking. Read it often to remember what is really important to a child of divorce.

2.15   Nobody in our family has ever been divorced and I feel really ashamed. Will my children feel the same way?

Making a change in how you see your family identity is huge for you. The best way to help your children is to establish a sense of pride in their new family and to look forward to the future with a real sense of possibility.

Your children will have an opportunity to witness you overcoming obstacles, demonstrating independence, and moving forward in your life notwithstanding challenges. You can be a great teacher to them during this time by demonstrating pride in your family and in yourself.

2.16   I am terrified of having my deposition taken. My spouse's lawyer is very aggressive, and I'm afraid I'm going to say something that will hurt my case.

A *deposition* is when you are asked a series of questions before a court reporter by the opposing attorney. The questions and your answers will be typed by the court reporter into a transcript that you will later be asked to read and sign. The purpose of the deposition is to gather information, assess you as a witness, and to commit you to certain positions in advance of trial. However, it is also an opportunity for you to assess the questioning techniques of your spouse's lawyer, determine the questions that you will likely be asked at trial, and a chance for you to practice what it will be like at the time of trial.

Feeling anxious about your deposition is normal. However, regardless of the personality of the lawyers, most depositions in divorces are quite uneventful. Remember that your attorney will be seated by your side at all times to support you. Ask to meet with your lawyer in advance to prepare for the deposition. If you are worried about certain questions that might be asked, talk to your attorney about them. Think of it as an opportunity, and enlist your lawyer's support in being well prepared. Chapter 5 explains the deposition process in more detail. Understanding the deposition process will help you feel more prepared.

2.17 **I am still so angry at my spouse. How can I be expected to sit in the same room during a settlement conference?**

A *settlement conference* is an opportunity to try and resolve some or all of the issues in your case without the necessity of a trial. Most settlement conferences, assuming you are represented by an attorney, are not done in the same room. Rather, the process resembles more of a "shuttle" negotiation. With this method, you and your attorney remain in one room while your spouse and his or her attorney are in another. Settlement offers are then relayed between the attorneys or the settlement conference judge or mediator throughout the negotiation process. By shifting your focus from your angry feelings to your goal of a settlement, it may be easier to proceed through the process.

2.18 **I'm afraid I can't make it through court without having an emotional breakdown. How do I prepare?**

Many people are eager to finalize their divorce; however, if it cannot be settled amicably out of court, the thought of going to trial can be frightening. It is not unusual to have concerns about the court process and how to prepare for the trial emotionally. Many people have never been in a courtroom, and their entire understanding of trial is based on what they have seen on television or heard from friends. A divorce trial can be a highly emotional experience. If your divorce case is going to trial, here are a few ideas that may help you through the process:

- Meet with your lawyer in advance of your court date to prepare you for court and the order of the trial testimony.

- Ask your lawyer whether there are any documents you should review in preparation for court, such as your deposition.

- Visit the courtroom in advance to get comfortable with the surroundings.

- Ask your lawyer about having a support person with you on your court date.

- Ask yourself what is the worst thing that could happen and consider what options you would have if it did.

- Avoid alcohol, eat healthfully, exercise, and have plenty of rest during the period of time leading up to the court date. Each of these will help you to prepare for the emotions of the day.
- Plan what you intend to wear in advance. Small preparations will lower your stress.
- Visualize the experience going well. Picture yourself sitting in the witness chair, giving clear, confident, and truthful answers to easy questions.
- Arrive early at the courthouse and make sure you have a plan for parking your car if you are not familiar with the area.
- Take slow, deep breaths. Breathing deeply will steady your voice, calm your nerves, and improve your focus.

Your attorney will be prepared to support you throughout the proceedings. By taking these steps, you can increase the ease of your experience. If even with these steps it is difficult for you emotionally, do not worry about it. Everyone, including the judge, understands this is an emotional time, and if necessary, your attorney will simply ask that a break be taken so that you have time to regain your composure.

2.19   I am really confused. One day I think the divorce is a mistake; the next day I know I can't go back, and a few minutes later I can hardly wait to be single again. Some days I just don't believe I'm getting divorced. What's happening?

Denial, transition, and acceptance are common passages for a person going through a divorce. What can be helpful to remember is that you may not pass from one stage to the next in a direct line. Feelings of anger or sadness may well up in you long after you thought you had moved on. Similarly, your mood might feel bright one day as you think about your future plans, even though you still miss your spouse.

Taking good care of yourself is essential during this period of your life. What you are going through requires a tremendous amount of energy. Allow yourself to experience your emotions, but also continue moving forward with your life. These steps will help your life get easier day by day.

3

Working with an Attorney

If there is one thing you can be sure of in your divorce, it's that you will be given plenty of advice. Well-intentioned neighbors, family members, and complete strangers will be happy to tell you war stories about their ex-spouse or about their sister who got divorced in another state. Many will insist they know what you should do, even though they know nothing about the facts of your case or the law in Arizona.

Every family, and therefore, every divorce, is different. Relying on what happened in your friend's divorce is not a recipe to follow for your divorce. So, thank them for the information, but keep in mind that any advice you take should come from your lawyer. Your lawyer should be your trusted and supportive advocate at all times throughout your divorce. The advice you receive from your attorney can affect your life for years to come. You will never regret taking the time and energy to choose the right lawyer for you.

See your relationship with your attorney as a partnership for pursuing what is most important to you. With clear and open attorney-client communication, you'll have the best outcome possible and your entire divorce will be less stressful.

By working closely with the right lawyer, you can trust the professional advice you receive and feel confident that you are pursuing the right path.

3.1 Where do I begin looking for an attorney for my divorce?

There are many ways to find a divorce lawyer. Ask people you trust—friends and family members who have gone through a divorce, if they thought they had a good lawyer (or if their former spouse did!). If you know professionals who work with attorneys, ask for a referral to an attorney who is experienced in family law. Consult your local bar association to find out whether they have a referral service. Be sure to specify that you are looking for an attorney who handles divorces. The State Bar of Arizona has list of attorneys who specialize in family law.

In addition, many attorneys have websites that provide information on their practice areas, professional associations, experience, and philosophy. However, be careful about reviews you read online. The reviews are often posted anonymously and therefore can be by non-clients (or the spouses of clients). Therefore, a negative review (or even a positive review) does not mean that the attorney is either right or wrong for you.

3.2 How do I choose the right attorney?

Choosing the right attorney for your divorce is an important decision. Your attorney should be a trusted professional with whom you feel comfortable sharing information openly. He or she should be a person you can trust and someone who will be a zealous advocate for your interests. However, he or she also needs to be someone who will advise you of the pros and cons so you can make informed choices.

You will rely upon your attorney to help you make many decisions throughout the course of your divorce. You will also entrust your legal counsel to make a range of strategic and procedural decisions on your behalf.

Consultation for a divorce might be your first meeting with a lawyer. Know that attorneys want to be supportive and to fully inform you. Feel free to seek all of the information you need to help you feel secure in knowing you have made the right choice.

Find an attorney who practices primarily in the family law area. Although many attorneys handle divorces, it is likely you will have more effective representation at a lower cost from an attorney who already knows the fundamentals of divorce law in Arizona.

Determine the level of experience you want in your attorney. For example, if you have had a short marriage, have no children and few assets, an attorney with lesser experience might be a good value for your legal needs. However, if you are anticipating a parenting time dispute or have complex or substantial assets, a more experienced attorney may better meet your needs. The State Bar of Arizona certifies attorneys who specialize in family law. If your case is complex, you may want to retain an attorney who is certified by the State Bar of Arizona as a family law specialist.

Consider the qualities in an attorney that are important to you. Even the most experienced and skilled attorney is not right for every person. Ask yourself what you are really looking for in an attorney so you can make your choice with these standards in mind. Your attorney is going to be learning more details about your life and marriage than most of your friends and family members. It is important the attorney you choose is someone with whom you feel comfortable discussing the personal details of your marriage.

Determine how the attorney likes to communicate with clients. Is it important to you to have an attorney who is available by e-mail after hours and on weekends? Does the attorney provide you his or her cell phone or a way for you to contact them if you need to reach them when the office is closed? Do you feel comfortable with the legal assistants or paralegals who will be helping the attorney with your case?

It is important that you have confidence in the attorney you hire. If you're unsure about whether the lawyer is really listening to you or understanding your concerns, keep looking until you find one who you can feel understands your needs. Your divorce is an important matter. It's critical that you have a professional you can trust.

A list of questions to consider in choosing a lawyer is included in the Appendix.

3.3   Should I interview more than one attorney?

Be willing to interview more than one attorney. Every lawyer has different strengths, and it is important that you find the one who is right for you. Sometimes it is only by meeting with more than one attorney that you clearly understand who will best be able to help you reach your goals in the way you want. Changing lawyers in the middle of litigation can be stressful and costly. It is wise to invest energy at the outset in making the right choice.

3.4 My spouse says that because we're still friends we should use the same attorney for the divorce. Is this a good idea?

One attorney cannot represent both parties. An attorney is ethically prohibited from representing two people with conflicting interests who are in dispute. The parties can attempt mediation without the use of attorneys, but the mediator cannot give legal advice to either party. The mediator can only assist the two parties to come to an agreement.

Sometimes couples have reached agreements without understanding all of their rights under the law. Even if everything can be resolved between the parties, you may still benefit from receiving at least some legal advice on matters such as tax considerations, retirement, and health insurance issues.

If your spouse has filed for divorce and said that you do not need an attorney, you should nevertheless meet with a lawyer for advice on how proceeding without a lawyer could affect your legal rights. This is an important decision that will result in a legally binding contract. Signing a contract without at least having a consultation with a lawyer or having a lawyer review the agreement may cause you to waive and give up important legal rights.

3.5 What information should I take with me to the first meeting with my attorney?

Attorneys differ on the amount of information they like to see at an initial consultation. When setting up the appointment, ask what documents you should bring to the first meeting. Often the legal assistant prior to the meeting will gather some preliminary information such as date of marriage, names of children, and occupations.

If your spouse has already filed for divorce or either you or your spouse has obtained an order of protection, it is important to take copies of any court documents. Other documents that you may be asked to bring include:

- Prenuptial or postnuptial agreement
- Will or trust agreements
- Last tax return
- Recent pay stubs
- Bank statements

If your situation is urgent or you do not have access to these documents, don't let it stop you from scheduling your appointment with an attorney. Prompt legal advice about your rights is often more important than having detailed financial information in the beginning. Your attorney can explain to you the options for obtaining these financial records if they are not readily available to you.

3.6 What unfamiliar words might an attorney use at the first meeting?

There are special terms used throughout a divorce proceeding that you will hear, and oftentimes as practitioners we forget that the terms, while familiar to us, are not familiar to you. The following is a list of frequently used terms. The definitions are not meant to be a substitute for a more thorough explanations of the processes involved in your proceeding. However, this will give you an overview of some of the terms you might hear during the divorce process. Additional terms are listed in the Glossary.

- *Dissolution of marriage*—the divorce
- *Community property*—property acquired during the marriage except property acquired by (1) gift, devise or descent or (2) acquired after service of a petition for dissolution of marriage, legal separation, or annulment
- *Petitioner* and *respondent*—In Arizona dissolution of marriage actions are not between plaintiffs and defendants. Rather the first person filing the papers is called the *petitioner* and the person responding is called the *respondent*. It does not matter in a

41

dissolution of marriage action if you are the petitioner or the respondent. The end result will be the same.

- *Qualified domestic relations order (QDRO)*—An order that is entered in cases where retirement plans must be divided.

- *Resolution management conference*—A court proceeding set by the court that you, your spouse, and your respective attorneys, if represented, will appear before the court. This is the court's first opportunity to meet the parties and see if there are any agreements between the parties. The court will set a trial date for all issues not resolved at the resolution management conference.

- *Temporary orders*—orders that a judge may make in your case prior to the time your divorce is finalized

3.7 What can I expect at an initial consultation with an attorney?

Sometimes attorneys will ask you to complete a questionnaire prior to the meeting. If they do not have you complete a questionnaire ahead of time, the first few minutes of the consultation will be used to obtain background information. With few exceptions, attorneys are required to keep confidential all information you provide.

The nature of the advice you get from an attorney in an initial consultation will depend upon whether you are still deciding whether you want a divorce, whether you are planning for a possible divorce in the future, or whether you are ready to file for divorce right away.

During the meeting, you will have an opportunity to provide the following information to the attorney:

- A brief history of the marriage
- Background information regarding yourself, your spouse, and your children
- Your immediate situation
- Your intentions and goals regarding your relationship with your spouse
- What information you are seeking from the attorney during the consultation

You can expect the attorney to identify the following information to you:

- The procedure for divorce in Arizona
- Identify the issues important in your case
- A preliminary assessment of your rights and responsibilities under the law
- Background information regarding the firm
- Information about fees and filings

Although some questions may be impossible for the attorney to answer at the initial consultation because additional information or research is needed, the initial consultation is an opportunity for you to ask all of the questions you have at the time of the meeting. This is also an opportunity for you to determine whether the attorney is someone you will have confidence in representing you.

3.8 Will the communication with my attorney be confidential?

Yes. Your lawyer has an ethical duty to maintain your confidentiality. This duty of confidentiality also extends to the legal staff working with your attorney. The privileged information that you share with your attorney will remain private and confidential, unless such privilege is waived by voluntarily disclosing it to third parties.

3.9 Is there any way that I could waive the attorney-client privilege, as it relates to the duty of confidentiality?

Yes. To ensure that communications between you and your attorney remain confidential, and to protect against the voluntary or involuntary waiver of such privilege, here are some tips to consider:

- Refrain from disclosing the content of the communications with your attorney or discussing in substantive detail the communications with your attorney with third parties. Such third parties can include friends and family members.
- Social media provides the potential for waiving the attorney-client privilege by publicly disclosing confi-

dential information. Do not post information or send messages relating to your case on Facebook, Twitter, or other social media websites.

- Do not post information relating to your case or communications with your attorney on a personal blog, video blog, online chat rooms, or online message boards.

- Do not use your work-related e-mail to communicate with your attorney or to discuss your case if others have access to the communication.

- Depending upon your employer's policy relating to electronic communication, the attorney-client privilege may be waived by communicating with your attorney or by discussing your case through your personal e-mail account (Gmail, Yahoo, etc.) via a company computer. To ensure your communications remain confidential, it is best to communicate only via e-mail from your private e-mail address from your home computer.

3.10 Can I take a friend or family member to my initial consultation?

Yes. Having someone present during your initial consultation can be a source of great support. You might ask him or her to take notes on your behalf so that you can focus on listening and asking questions. Remember that this is your consultation, however, and it is important that the attorney hears the facts of your case directly from you. Also, ask your attorney how having a third-party present at your consultation could impact the attorney-client privilege. You should *never,* however, bring your children with you to the consultation.

3.11 What exactly will my attorney do to help me get a divorce?

Your attorney will play a critical role in helping you get your divorce. You will be actively involved in some of the work, while other actions will be taken behind the scenes at the law office.

Your attorney may perform any of the following tasks on your behalf:

- Assess the case to determine which court is the proper court to hear your divorce.
- Develop a strategy for advising you about all aspects of your divorce, including the treatment of assets and matters concerning children.
- Prepare legal documents for filing with the court.
- Conduct discovery to obtain information from the other party, which could include depositions, requests for production of documents, and written interrogatories.
- Appear with you at all court appearances, depositions, and conferences.
- Schedule all deadlines and court appearances.
- Support you in responding to information requests from your spouse.
- Inform you of actions you are required to take.
- Perform financial analyses of your case.
- Conduct legal research.
- Prepare you for court appearances and depositions.
- Prepare your case for hearings and trial, including preparing exhibits and interviewing witnesses.
- Advise you regarding your rights under the law.
- Counsel you regarding the risks and benefits of negotiated settlement as compared to proceeding to trial.

As your advocate, your attorney is entrusted to take all of the steps necessary to represent your interests in the divorce.

3.12 What professionals should I expect to work with during my divorce?

Depending upon the issues identified by your attorney, you can expect to work with various types of professionals, such as business valuators, forensic accountants, financial professionals, real estate agents, and mental health experts.

Additionally, in some cases where legal decision-making or parenting time issues are seriously disputed, the court may, in addition to appointing a mental health professional to conduct an assessment of parenting time, also appoint a court appointed advisor, a best interest attorney or a children's attorney. Each of these persons has a slightly different role.

The mental health professional is generally a doctor of psychology. The scope of the mental health provider's role will depend upon the purpose for which she or he was appointed. For example, the psychologist may be appointed to perform a *parenting time evaluation,* which involves assessing both parents and the child, or this expert may be ordered to evaluate one parent to assess the child's safety while spending time with that parent.

The court appointed advisor is someone who may do a specific investigation and advise the trial judge about the results of the investigation. Sometimes this investigation may be very specific, such as investigating an allegation that the father does not have a pool fence. Other times, the court may want the court advisor to talk with both parents about parenting time arrangements and report back to the court.

The best interest attorney is an attorney appointed by the court and has the duty to represent the best interest of the child. The best interest attorney will investigate you and your spouse as well as the needs of your child. She or he may then be called as a witness at trial to testify regarding any relevant observations.

A children's attorney represents the child and advocates, just as any other attorney in the case, for his or her client's position.

3.13 I've been divorced before and I don't think I need an attorney this time; however, my spouse is hiring one. Is it wise to go it alone?

Having gone through a prior divorce, it's likely that you have learned a great deal about the divorce process as well as your legal rights. However, there are many reasons why you should be extremely cautious about proceeding without legal representation.

It is important to remember that every divorce is different. The length of the marriage, whether there are children, the relative financial situation of you and your spouse, as well as your age and health can all affect the financial outcome in your divorce.

The law may have changed since your last divorce. Some aspects of divorce law are likely to change each year. New laws get passed and new decisions get handed down by the Arizona Supreme Court and the Arizona Court of Appeals that affect the rights and responsibilities of people who divorce. In some cases, the involvement of your lawyer could be minimal. This might be the case if your marriage was short, your financial situation very similar to that of your spouse, there are no children, and the two of you remain amicable. At a minimum, have an initial consultation with an attorney to discuss your rights and have an attorney review any final agreement.

3.14   Can I bring my children to meetings with my attorney?

It's best to make other arrangements for your children when you meet with your attorney. Your attorney will be giving you a great deal of important information during your conferences, and it will benefit you to give your full attention.

It's also recommended that you take every measure to keep information about the legal aspects of your divorce away from your children. Knowledge that you are seeing an attorney can add to your child's anxiety about the process. It can also make your child a target for questioning by the other parent about your contacts with your attorney.

Most law offices are not designed to accommodate young children and are ordinarily not "child-proof." For both your child's well-being and your own peace of mind, explore options for someone to care for your child when you have meetings with your attorney.

3.15   What is the role of the *paralegal* or *legal assistant* in my attorney's office?

A *paralegal,* or *legal assistant,* is a trained legal professional whose duties include providing support for you and your lawyer. Working with a paralegal can make your divorce easier because he or she is likely to be very available to help you. It can also lower your legal costs, as the hourly rate for paralegal services is less than the rate for attorneys.

A paralegal is prohibited from giving legal advice. It is important that you respect the limits of the role of the paralegal if he or she is unable to answer your question because it calls for giving a legal opinion. However, a paralegal can answer many questions about the status of your case and provide a great deal of information from the attorney to you throughout your divorce.

Paralegals can help you by receiving information from you, reviewing documents with you, providing you with updates on your case, and answering questions about the divorce process that do not call for legal advice.

3.16 My attorney is not returning my phone calls. What can I do?

You have a right to expect your phone calls to be returned by your lawyer. Here are some options to consider:

- Ask to speak to the paralegal or another attorney in the office.

- Send an e-mail or fax telling your lawyer that you have been trying to reach him or her by phone and explaining the reason it is important that you receive a call.

- Ask the receptionist or secretary to schedule a phone conference for you to speak with your attorney at a specific date and time.

- Schedule a meeting with your attorney to discuss both the issue needing attention as well as your concerns about the communication.

Your attorney wants to provide good service to you. If your calls are not being returned, take action to get the communication with your lawyer back on track.

3.17 How do I know when it's time to change lawyers?

Changing lawyers is costly. You will incur legal fees for your new attorney to review information that is already familiar to your current attorney. You will spend time giving much of the same information to your new lawyer that you gave to the one you have discharged. A change in lawyers often results in delays in the divorce.

The following are questions to ask yourself when you're deciding whether to stay with your attorney or seek new counsel:

- Have I spoken directly to my attorney about my concerns?
- When I expressed concerns, did my lawyer take action accordingly?
- Is my lawyer open and receptive to what I have to say?
- Am I blaming my lawyer for bad behavior of my spouse or opposing counsel?
- Have I provided my lawyer the information needed for taking the next action?
- Does my lawyer have control over the complaints I have, or are they ruled by the law or the judge?
- Is my lawyer keeping promises for completing action on my case?
- Do I trust my lawyer?
- What would be the advantages of changing lawyers when compared to the cost?
- Do I believe my lawyer will support me to achieve the outcome I'm seeking in my divorce?

Every effort should be made to resolve concerns with your attorney. If you have made this effort and the situation remains unchanged, it may be time to switch lawyers.

3.18   Are there certain expectations that I should have when working with my legal team?

Yes, your legal team will be able to provide you with support and guidance during this process. There are certain actions you can expect your legal team to do for you during your divorce. A list of some of them follows.

Meet with you prior to the filing of a court action to advise you on actions you should take first. There may be important steps to take before you initiate the legal process. Your legal team can support you to be well prepared prior to initiating divorce.

Take action to obtain a temporary court order or to enforce existing orders. Temporary court orders are often needed to ensure clarity regarding rights and responsibilities while your divorce is pending. Your legal team can help you obtain a temporary order and ask the court to enforce its orders if there is a violation.

Explain the legal process during each step of your case. Understanding the legal process reduces the stress of your divorce. Your legal team can guide you each step of the way.

Listen to your concerns and answer any questions. Although only the attorneys can give you legal advice, everyone on your team is available to listen, to provide support, and to direct you to the right person who can help.

Support you in developing your parenting plan. Many parents do not know how to decide what type of parenting plan is best for their children. Your legal team can help you look at the needs of your children and offer advice based on their experience in working with families.

Support you in the completion of your discovery responses and preparing for depositions. The discovery process can be overwhelming for anyone. You will be asked to provide detailed information and many documents. Your legal team can make this job easier. Just ask. If your case involves depositions, your legal team will support you to be fully prepared for the experience.

Identify important issues, analyze the evidence, and advise you. Divorce is complex. Often there is a great deal of uncertainty. Your legal team can analyze the unique facts of your case and advise you based upon the law and their expertise.

Communicate with the opposing party's attorney to try to resolve issues without going to court and to keep your case progressing. Although your attorney cannot control the actions of the opposing party or their lawyer, your attorney can always initiate communication as your advocate. Phoning, e-mailing, or writing to opposing counsel are actions your legal team can take to encourage cooperation and to keep your divorce moving forward at the pace you want without the expense of contested litigation.

Think creatively regarding challenges with your case and provide options for your consideration. At the outset, you may see many obstacles to reaching a final resolution. Your legal team can offer creative ideas for resolving challenges and help you to explore your options to achieve the best possible outcome.

Facilitate the settlement process. Although your legal team can never make the other party settle, your attorney can take action to promote settlement. They can prepare settlement proposals, invite settlement conferences, and negotiate zealously on your behalf.

3.19 Are there certain things my legal team will not be able to do?

Yes. Although there are many ways in which your legal team can support you during your divorce, there are also things your legal team will not be able to accomplish.

Force the other parent to exercise their parenting time. Your legal team cannot force a parent to exercise parenting time. However, be mindful that a chronic neglect of parenting time may be a basis for modifying your parenting plan. Tell your attorney if the other parent is repeatedly failing to exercise their parenting time.

Force the other party to respond to a settlement proposal. Your attorney may send proposals or make requests to opposing counsel; however, there is no duty to respond. After repeated follow-ups without a response, it may be clear no response is coming. At that time, your attorney will decide whether the issues merit court action. Both parties must agree on all terms for a case to be settled without a trial. If one party wants to proceed to trial, even over a single issue, he or she will be able to do so.

Control the tone of communication from opposing counsel or communications from the other party or the other party's family members. Unfortunately, communication from the opposing attorney may sometimes appear rude, condescending, or demanding. Your legal team cannot stop an attorney from using these tactics.

Absent a pattern of harassment or if an order of protection is in effect, your legal team cannot stop your spouse from contacting you. If you do not want the contact, talk with your attorney about how to best handle the situation. Of course, appropriate communication regarding your children is always encouraged. *Ask the court to compensate you for every wrong done to you by the other party over the course of your marriage.* Although your attorney will empathize that you do have valid complaints, please understand that focusing on the most important issues will yield the best outcome in the end. Raising numerous small issues may distract from your most important goals.

Remedy poor financial decisions made during the marriage. With few exceptions, the court's duty is to divide the marital estate as it currently exists. The judge will not attempt to remedy all past financial wrongs, such as overspending or poor investments by your spouse. If there is significant debt, consult with a debt counselor or bankruptcy lawyer.

Control how the other party parents your children during his or her parenting time. Each parent has strengths and weaknesses. Absent special needs of a child, most judges will not issue orders regarding bedtimes, amount of TV watching or playing video games, discipline methods, clothing, or diet. Of course, any suspected abuse should be reported immediately to the appropriate authorities.

Demand an accounting of how a parent uses court ordered child support. Absent extraordinary circumstances, the court will not order the other parent to provide an accounting for the use of child support.

Leveraging money for rights regarding your children. Tactics oriented toward asserting parenting rights as leverage toward attaining financial goals will be discouraged. Your legal team should negotiate parenting issues based solely on considerations related to the best interest of your child, then separately negotiate the financial considerations.

Guaranteed timely payment of child support and spousal maintenance. Enforcement of payment of support is only possible when it is court ordered. However, even with a court order, you may experience inconsistent timing of payment due to job loss or a refusal to pay. Talk with your attorney if a pattern of repeated missed payments has developed.

Collect child-care and uninsured medical expenses if provisions of the decree are not complied with. If your decree requires you to provide documentation of payment of expenses to the other party and you fail to, you could be prohibited from collecting reimbursement for those expenses. Follow the court's orders regarding providing documentation to the other parent, even if they don't pay as they should. Always keep records of these expenses and payments made by each parent, and keep copies of communications with the other parent regarding payment/reimbursement. It is much easier to keep these records on an ongoing basis than to get copies of old checks, day-care bills, medical bills, and insurance documents at a later time.

4

Attorney's Fees and Costs

Anytime you make a major investment, you want to know what the cost is going to be and what you are getting for your money. Investing in quality legal representation for your divorce is no different.

The cost of your divorce might be one of your greatest concerns. Because of this, you will want to be an intelligent consumer of legal services. You want quality, but you also want to get the best value for the fees you are paying.

Legal fees for a divorce can be costly and the total expense not always predictable. But there are many actions you can take to control and estimate the cost. Develop a plan early on for how you will finance your divorce. Speak openly with your lawyer about fees from the outset. Learn as much as you can about how you will be charged. You will be asked to sign a written fee agreement. Read it carefully and ask questions.

By being informed, aware, and wise, your financial investment in your divorce will be money well spent to protect your future.

4.1   Can I get free legal advice from a lawyer over the phone?

Every law firm has its own policy regarding lawyers talking to people who are not yet clients of the firm. Most questions about your divorce are too complex for a lawyer to give a meaningful answer during a brief phone call.

Questions about your divorce require a complete look at the facts, circumstances, and background of your marriage.

To obtain good legal advice, it's best to schedule an initial consultation with a lawyer who handles divorces.

4.2 Will I be charged for an initial consultation with a lawyer?

It depends. Some lawyers give free consultations, while others charge a fee. When scheduling your appointment, you should be told the amount of the fee. Payment is ordinarily due at the time of the consultation. Sometimes, all you may need is an initial consultation. Accordingly, paying a fee now for an hour consultation may save you lots of money in the future.

4.3 If I decide to hire an attorney, when do I have to pay him or her?

If your attorney charges for an initial consultation, be prepared to make payment at the time of your meeting. At the close of your consultation, the attorney may tell you the amount of the retainer needed by the law firm to handle your divorce. However, you are not expected to pay the retainer at the time of your first meeting. Rather, the retainer is paid after you have decided to hire the lawyer, the lawyer has accepted your case, and you are ready to proceed.

4.4 What exactly is a *retainer* and how much will mine be?

A *retainer* is a sum paid to your lawyer in advance as a deposit for services to be performed and costs to be incurred in your divorce. This amount will be an advance credit for services that will be charged by the hour.

If your case is accepted by the law firm, expect the attorney to request a retainer following the initial consultation. The amount of the retainer may vary from hundreds of dollars to several thousand dollars, depending upon the nature of your case. Contested cases that require going to court, divorces involving businesses, or interstate custody disputes between parents, for example, are all likely to require higher retainers.

Other factors that can affect the amount of the retainer include the nature and number of the disputed issues.

4.5 Will my attorney accept my divorce case on a contingency-fee basis?

No. A *contingency fee* is one that becomes payable only if your case is successful. Your lawyer may not accept payment based upon securing your divorce, the amount of support awarded, or the division of the property settlement.

4.6 How much does it cost to get a divorce?

The cost of your divorce will depend upon many factors. Most attorneys charge by the hour for divorces. Accordingly, if your case is relatively simple and it can be resolved amicably or in mediation, the costs will be substantially less than if the lawyer has to bring proceedings in court. Any time you have to go to court the amount of time involved is greater and therefore your costs will be higher.

It is important that your discussion of the cost of your divorce begins at your first meeting with your attorney. It is customary for family law attorneys to request a retainer, also known as a *fee advance,* prior to beginning work on your case.

Be sure to ask your attorney what portion, if any, of the retainer is refundable if you do not continue with the case or if you terminate your relationship with the attorney. Also ask whether there are paralegals or more junior attorneys who work in the office who might be able to do some of the work to help keep costs down.

It may also be possible to receive a portion of your attorney's fees from your spouse if you are the non-working spouse or there is a substantial disparity in income.

4.7 If I can't afford to pay the full amount of the retainer, can I make monthly payments to my attorney?

Every law firm has its own policies regarding payment arrangements for divorce clients. Often these arrangements are tailored to the specific client. Most attorneys will require a substantial retainer to be paid at the outset of your case. Some attorneys may accept monthly payments in lieu of the retainer. Most will require monthly payments in addition to the initial retainer or request additional retainers as your case progresses. Ask frank questions of your attorney to be clear about your responsibility for payment of legal fees.

4.8 I agreed to pay my attorney a substantial retainer to begin my case. Will I still have to make monthly payments?

Ask your attorney what will be expected of you regarding payments on your account while the divorce is in progress. Clarify whether monthly payments on your account will be expected, whether it is likely that you will be asked to pay additional retainers, and whether the firm charges interest on past due accounts. Regular payments to your attorney can help you avoid having a tremendously burdensome legal bill at the end of your case. Additionally, you may also be required to keep a minimum credit balance on your account to ensure your case is adequately funded for ongoing work by your legal team.

4.9 Can I recover my attorney's fees from my spouse if I am not working?

Under Arizona law, attorney's fees may be awarded to the non-working spouse or to the spouse who has less income due to the substantial disparity between the spouses in income. Your attorney may recommend obtaining temporary orders for attorney's fees so that you can have sufficient funds to pay your attorney and retain any experts needed for your case.

4.10 My lawyer gave me an estimate of the cost of my divorce and it sounds reasonable. Do I still need a written fee agreement?

Absolutely. This is essential not only to define the scope of the services for which you have hired your lawyer, but also to ensure that you have a clear understanding about matters such as your attorney's hourly rate, whether you will be billed for certain costs such as copying, and when you can expect to receive statements on your account.

A clear fee agreement reduces the risk of misunderstandings between you and your lawyer. It supports you both in being clear about your promises to each other so that your focus can be on the legal services being provided rather than on disputes about your fees.

4.11 How will I know how the fees and charges are accumulating?

Be sure your written fee agreement with your attorney is completely clear about how you will be informed regarding the status of your account. You should receive a monthly statement of the services performed and how much of your retainer you have remaining as well as how much you have been charged for the services performed.

Review the statement of your account promptly after you receive it. Check to make sure there are no errors, such as duplicate billing entries. If your statement reflects work that you were unaware was performed, call for clarification. Your attorney's office should welcome any questions you have about services it provided.

Your statement might also include filing fees, court reporter fees for transcripts of court testimony or depositions, copy expenses, or interest charged on your account. If several weeks have passed and you have not received a statement on your account, call your attorney's office to request one. Legal fees can mount quickly, and it is important that you stay aware of the status of your legal expenses.

4.12 What other expenses are related to the divorce litigation besides lawyer fees?

Talk to your attorney about costs other than the attorney fees. There will be filing fees payable to the court for filing the petition of dissolution as well as responding. If you have children, you will also pay a fee to attend a parenting class. Ask whether it is likely there will be other fees owed to the court, court reporter expenses, subpoenas, expert-witness fees, or costs for a mediator. Expert-witness fees can be a substantial expense, ranging into thousands of dollars, depending upon the type of expert and the extent to which he or she is involved in your case.

Speak frankly with your attorney about these costs so that together you can make the best decisions about how to use your budget for the litigation.

4.13 Who pays for the experts such as appraisers, accountants, psychologists, and mediators?

Costs for the services of experts, whether appointed by the court or hired by the parties, are ordinarily paid for by the parties. However, depending upon the circumstances, one party can be ordered to pay the entire fee, or you and your spouse may agree to pay the fees jointly out of community funds.

Psychologists or other mental health providers who may be asked to perform a *parenting time evaluation* (formerly referred to as a *custody evaluation*) or a limited assessment focused on particular issue usually charge by the hour or set a flat fee for a certain type of evaluation. Again, the court can order one party to pay this fee or both parties to share the expense. It is not uncommon for a psychologist to request payment in advance and hold the release of an expert report until fees are paid.

Mediators either charge a flat fee per session or an hourly rate fee. Generally, each party will pay one-half of the mediator's fee, which is paid prior to your mediation sessions.

The fees for many experts, including appraisers and accountants, will vary depending upon whether the individuals are called upon to provide only a specific service such as an appraisal or whether they will need to prepare for giving testimony and appear as a witness at trial.

4.14 What factors will impact how much my divorce will cost?

Although it is difficult to predict how much your legal fees will be, the following are some of the factors that affect the cost:

- Whether there are children
- Whether parenting time (child custody) is agreed upon
- Whether there is a community business to be valued
- Whether one spouse is a professional and has goodwill to be valued
- Whether a pension plan will be divided between the parties
- The nature of the issues contested

- The number of issues agreed to by the parties
- The cooperation of the opposing party and opposing counsel
- The frequency of your communication with your legal team
- The ability of the parties to communicate with each other without the need to involve lawyers in all communications
- The promptness with which information is provided or exchanged between both the clients and the attorneys
- Whether there are litigation costs, such as fees for expert witnesses or court reporters
- The hourly rate of the attorney
- The time it will take to conclude your divorce

Communicating with your lawyer regularly about your legal fees will help you to have a better understanding of the overall cost as your case proceeds.

4.15   Will my attorney charge for phone calls and e-mails?

You should expect to be billed for any communication with your attorney. Many of the professional services provided by lawyers are done by phone and by e-mail. This time can be spent giving legal advice, negotiating, or gathering information to protect your interests. These calls and e-mails are all legal services for which you should anticipate being charged by your attorney.

To make the most of your time during attorney phone calls, plan your call in advance. Organize the information you want to relay, your questions, and any concerns to be addressed. This will help you to be clear and focused during the phone call so that your fees are well spent. It is best to save your questions and comments for one complete e-mail or telephone conversation. Multiple communications, even if just short questions, will increase the cost of your services.

4.16   Will I be charged for talking to the staff at my lawyer's office?

Whether you are charged fees for talking to non-lawyers in the law office may depend upon their role in the office. For example, most law firms charge for the services of paralegals and law clerks. Generally, a legal assistant, secretary, or receptionist who will just be taking information or setting appointments will not charge for services.

Remember that non-lawyers cannot give legal advice, so it is important to respect their roles. Don't expect the receptionist to give you an opinion regarding whether you will win parenting time or receive spousal maintenance.

Your lawyer's support staff will be able to relay your messages and receive information from you. They may also be able to answer many of your questions. Allowing this type of support from within the firm is an important way to control your legal fees, too.

4.17   What is a *trial retainer* and will I have to pay one?

The purpose of the *trial retainer* is to fund the work needed to prepare for trial and for services on the day or days of trial. A trial retainer is a sum of money paid on your account with your lawyer when it appears as though your case may not settle and is at risk for proceeding to trial.

Confirm with your attorney that any unearned portion of your trial retainer will be refunded if your case settles. Ask your lawyer whether and when a trial retainer might be required in your case so that you can avoid surprises and plan your budget accordingly.

Not all lawyers charge trial retainers. Verify with your lawyer ahead of time whether a trial retainer will be required.

4.18   How do I know whether I should spend the attorney fees my lawyer says it will require to take my case to trial?

Deciding whether to take a case to trial or to settle is often the most challenging point in the divorce process. This decision should be made with the support of your attorney.

When the issues in dispute are primarily financial, often the decision about settlement is related to the costs of going to trial. It is worthwhile to determine just how far apart you and your spouse are on the financial matters and compare this to the estimated costs of going to trial. By comparing these amounts, you can decide whether a compromise on certain financial issues and certainty about the outcome would be better than paying legal fees and not knowing how your case will resolve. For example, if you know it is going to cost $20,000 to go to trial, and this is close to the amount your spouse is requesting to settle the matter, then spend the money settling and pay your spouse rather than paying your lawyer to take the matter to trial!

4.19 Is there any way I can reduce some of the expenses of getting a divorce?

Litigation of any kind can be expensive, and divorces are no exception. The good news is that there are many ways that you can help control the expense. Here are some of them.

Put it in writing. If you need to relay information that is important but not urgent, consider providing it to your attorney by mail, fax, or e-mail. This creates a prompt and accurate record for your file and takes less time than exchanging phone messages and talking on the phone.

Keep your attorney informed. Just as your attorney should keep you up to date on the status of your case, you need to do the same. Keep your lawyer advised about any major developments in your life such as plans to move, have someone move into your home, change your employment status, or buy or sell property.

During your divorce, if your contact information changes, be sure to notify your attorney. Your attorney may need to reach you with information, and reaching you in a timely manner may help avoid more costly fees later.

Obtain copies of documents. An important part of litigation includes reviewing documents such as tax returns, account statements, report cards, or medical records. Your attorney will ordinarily be able to request or subpoena these items, but many may be readily available to you directly upon request.

Utilize support professionals. Get to know the support staff at your lawyer's office. Although only attorneys are able to give you legal advice, the receptionist, paralegal, legal secretary, or law clerk may be able to answer your questions regarding the status of your case. All communication with any professionals in a law firm is required to be kept strictly confidential.

Leave a detailed message. If your attorney knows the information you are seeking, she or he can often get the answer before returning your call. This not only gets your answer faster, but also reduces costs.

Discuss more than one matter during a call. It is not unusual for clients to have many questions during litigation. If your question is not urgent, consider waiting to call until you have more than one inquiry. Never hesitate to call to ask any legal questions.

Provide timely responses to information requests. Whenever possible, provide information requested by your lawyer in a timely manner. This avoids the cost of follow-up action by your lawyer and the additional expense of extending the time in litigation.

Carefully review your monthly statements. Scrutinize your monthly billing statements closely. If you believe an error has been made, contact your lawyer's office right away to discuss your concerns.

Remain open to settlement. Be alert to recognize that when your disagreement concerns financial matters, the value of money in dispute may be less than the amount it will cost to go to trial. By doing your part, you can use your legal fees wisely and control the costs of your divorce.

4.20   I don't have any money and I need a divorce. What are my options?

If your case is relatively simple and straightforward you may not need a lawyer. You can obtain court approved forms from the superior court where you will be filing your divorce. The papers are sometimes available online; in other cases, they available in the clerk's office of your county's superior court. The Supreme Court's website also has self-service information.

In addition, by calling the Contact Clearinghouse Center at (602) 252-4045, you can obtain information about several legal organizations that offer free or reduced legal services. The organizations have different screening processes for potential clients and the demand for their services is great. If you believe you might be eligible for participation in one of these programs, inquire early to increase your opportunity to get the legal help you are seeking.

4.21 My spouse has money for an attorney, but I don't have any money, how can I obtain an attorney so I do not feel like I am at a disadvantage?

If you are concerned that your spouse is in control of the funds and has funds to purchase an attorney but you do not, consider the following:

- Talk with a lawyer about whether you can use joint funds you have with your spouse to retain a lawyer.

- Consider putting the initial retainer on a low interest credit card until your lawyer can either work with your spouse's lawyer to have your spouse provide you with the funds for a retainer or until the court enters temporary orders to provide you with sufficient funds to retain a lawyer.

- Borrow the legal fees from friends or family. Often those close to you are concerned about your future and would be pleased to support you in your goal of having your rights protected. Always make sure that the loan is in writing so that you have proof to show the court that you must pay it back.

- Start saving. If your case is not urgent, consider developing a plan for saving the money you need to proceed with a divorce. Your attorney may be willing to receive and hold monthly payments until you have paid an amount sufficient to pay the initial retainer.

- Ask your attorney about your spouse paying for your legal fees.

- Ask your attorney about being paid from the proceeds of the property settlement. If you and your spouse have acquired substantial assets during the marriage, you may be able to seek temporary orders to divide some of the assets prior to the conclusion of the divorce so that you may have funds, on a temporary basis, to pay a portion of your attorney's fees until a final resolution can be reached in court.

Closely examine all sources of funds readily available to you, as you may have overlooked money that might be easily accessible to you.

Even if you do not have the financial resources to proceed with your divorce at this time, consult with an attorney to learn your rights and to develop an action plan for steps you can take between now and the time you are able to proceed.

Often there are measures you can take right away to protect yourself until you have the money to proceed with your divorce.

4.22 Is there anything I can do on my own to get support for my children if I don't have money for a lawyer for a divorce?

Yes. If you need support for your children, contact the Arizona Department of Economic Security for help in obtaining a child support order. Although they cannot help you with matters such as parenting time or property division, they can pursue support from your spouse for your children.

You can visit the Arizona Department of Economic Security's website at (www.azdes.gov/az_child_support). The Division of Child Support Services holds many educational workshops throughout the year to assist in obtaining information about the services offered.

4.23 If my mother pays my legal fees, will my lawyer give her private information about my divorce?

No. Even if someone else pays your legal fees, you are the client, and no one else should receive information about your divorce.

If someone else is paying your legal feels, discuss with your lawyer and the payer your expectations that your lawyer will honor the ethical duty of confidentiality. Without your permission, your attorney should not disclose information to others about your case.

4.24 Can I ask the court to order my spouse to pay my attorney fees?

Yes. If you want to ask the court to order your spouse to pay any portion of your legal fees, be sure to discuss this with your attorney at the first opportunity. Most lawyers will treat the obligation for your legal fees as yours until the other party has made payment.

If your case is likely to require costly experts and your spouse has a much greater ability to pay these expenses than you, talk to your lawyer about the possibility of filing a motion for temporary orders with the court asking your spouse to pay toward these costs while the case is pending.

4.25 What happens if I don't pay my attorney the fees I promised to pay?

The ethical rules for lawyers allow your attorney to withdraw from representation if you do not comply with your fee agreement. Consequently, it is important that you keep the promises you have made regarding your account.

If you are having difficulty paying your attorney's fees, talk with your attorney about payment options. Consider borrowing the funds, using your credit card, or asking for help from friends and family.

Above all, do not avoid communication with your attorney if you are having challenges making payment. Keeping in touch with your attorney is essential for you to have an advocate at all stages of your divorce.

5

The Discovery Process

You have just filed for a divorce, and within a few days, the opposing party will send a list of documents that you need to produce. These documents may be from years earlier; and, you'll also receive *interrogatories*—documents that seek responses to questions that your spouse should already know. If you contact your lawyer and ask whether you really need to respond to the questions, the answer is: yes.

Discovery is one of the least talked about steps in divorce, but it is often among the most important. Discovery is the pre-trial phase in a lawsuit during which each party can obtain evidence from the opposing party. The purpose of discovery is to ensure that both you and your spouse have access to the same information. In this way, you can either negotiate a fair agreement or have all of the facts and documents to present to the judge at trial. The discovery process enables you and your spouse to meet on a more level playing field when it comes to settling your case or taking it to trial. You and your spouse both need the same information if you hope to reach agreement on any of the issues in your divorce. Similarly, a judge must know all of the facts to make a fair decision.

The discovery process may seem tedious at times because of the need to obtain and to provide lots of detailed information. Completing it, however, can give tremendous clarity about the issues in your divorce. Trust your lawyer's advice about the importance of having the necessary evidence as you complete the discovery process in order to reach your goals in your divorce.

5.1   What types of discovery might be done by my lawyer or my spouse's lawyer?

Types of discovery include:

- *Interrogatories*—written questions that must be answered under oath
- *Requests for production of documents*—asking that certain documents be provided by you or your spouse
- *Requests for admissions*—asking that certain facts be admitted or denied
- *Subpoena of documents*—asking for documents such as bank records, employment records, or medical records from third parties who are in possession of such documents
- *Depositions*—questions that are asked and answered in the presence of a court reporter but outside the presence of a judge

Factors that can influence the type of discovery conducted in your divorce can include:

- The types of issues in dispute
- How much access you and your spouse have to needed information
- The level of cooperation in sharing information
- The budget available for performing discovery

Talk to your lawyer about the nature and extent of discovery anticipated in your case.

5.2   Do I really have to provide all this information to my spouse when they already know this information?

It can almost seem harassing at times to think that you must respond in writing to questions that your spouse already knows or to produce documents about financial accounts that either party can easily obtain. However, remember that while your spouse may know this information, the lawyers for your spouse (and maybe even your lawyer) do not have all the information. By assembling the information now, it will help to educate all the participants and may help facilitate an early settlement.

The Arizona Rules of Family Law and Procedure also require that the parties exchange certain information voluntarily at the start of the case. This is often referred to as *disclosures under Rule 49*. Depending on the issues involved in your case, you will need to voluntarily exchange information about:

- Child support (income, insurance premiums, school expenses, expenses for the special needs of a child)
- Spousal maintenance (income)
- Property (deeds, purchase agreements, escrow documents, monthly financial account statements, retirement accounts, cash surrender value of life insurance, valuations, appraisals, tax returns, items of personal property)
- Debts (monthly or periodic statements showing debts owed, copies of credit card statements)
- Witnesses and expert witnesses

You have a continuing duty to disclose information when new or different information is discovered or revealed. Discuss your disclosure obligations early with your attorney so that you can promptly gather the necessary documents. Just keep in mind, this may seem like an unreasonable step, but it is a necessary part of the divorce process.

5.3   How long does the discovery process take?

Discovery can take anywhere from a few weeks to a number of months, depending upon factors such as the complexity of the case, the cooperation of you and your spouse, and whether expert witnesses are involved.

The Arizona Rules of Family Law and Procedure provide that interrogatories, requests for production of documents, and requests for admissions be responded to within forty days.

5.4   My lawyer insists that we conduct discovery, but I don't want to spend the time and money on it. Is it really necessary?

The discovery process can be critical to a successful outcome in your case for several reasons:

- It increases the likelihood that any agreements reached are based on accurate information.

- It provides necessary information for deciding whether to settle or proceed to trial.
- It supports the preparation of defenses that may be available in your case.
- It avoids surprises at trial, such as unexpected witness testimony.
- It ensures all potential issues are identified by your attorney.

Discuss with your attorney the intention behind the discovery being conducted in your case to ensure it is consistent with your goals and a meaningful investment of your legal fees.

5.5   I just received from my spouse's attorney interrogatories and requests that I produce documents. My lawyer wants me to respond within thirty days. I'll never make the deadline. What can I do?

Your lawyer is asking for the information before the deadline so that your lawyer has an opportunity to review the information before submitting the information to the other side. Answering your discovery promptly will help move your case forward and help control your legal fees. There are steps you can take to make this task easier.

First, look at all of the questions. Many of them will not apply or your answers will be a simple "yes" or "no." Some of them also may not be applicable, and others you may not have the information. It is alright to say "not applicable" or "information not known."

Ask a friend to help you. It is important that you develop the practice of letting others help you while you are going through your divorce. Chances are that you will make great progress in just a couple of hours with a friend helping you.

Break it down into smaller tasks. If you answer just a few questions a day, the job will not be so overwhelming.

Call your lawyer. Ask whether a paralegal in the office can help you organize the needed information or determine whether some of it can be provided at a later date.

Delay in the discovery process often leads to frustration by clients and lawyers. Do your best to provide the information in a timely manner with the help of others.

5.6 I don't have access to my documents and my spouse is being uncooperative in providing my lawyer with information. Can my lawyer request information directly from an employer or financial institution?

Yes, it may be possible to issue a subpoena directly to an employer or financial institution. A *subpoena* is a court order directing an individual or corporate representative to produce documents in a pending lawsuit. These documents may include such things as employment files, employment benefits, bank statements, or credit card statements. Your lawyer will discuss with you the types of documents that can be requested that will be relevant to the issues in your case.

5.7 My spouse's lawyer intends to subpoena my medical records. Aren't these private?

Some of the most private information about you is often contained in your medical records. However, medical records often become a contention in divorce especially if your spouse is insisting that you sign releases so the records can be produced as part of your required disclosure of information. Whether your medical records are relevant in your case will depend upon the issues in dispute. If you are requesting spousal support and are claiming you cannot work because of your medical condition, then your medical records may be relevant to show whether your medical condition prohibits you from working. In such cases, the court will probably require you to sign a release so the medical provider can release the documents.

If parenting time is in dispute and you or your spouse are claiming that a medical condition affects the ability to parent then medical records may be relevant. If either parent has seen a counselor or is in therapy, mental health records may also be relevant.

Talk with your lawyer about your rights. There are a number of options that may be available to keep or prevent the disclosure of your information. If the records are not relevant to any issue and are just being requested to harass you, then your lawyer may be able to obtain a protective order so that the records do not have to be disclosed or disclosure is limited.

In Arizona, a *confidentiality order* is available to restrict a party or person from disclosing information or documents to anyone outside the litigation. A party wishing to obtain a confidentiality order must either obtain a stipulation and agreement from the other party or seek a court order. To obtain a confidentiality order from the court, the court requires a party requesting such an order to show "good cause." Therefore, you, or your attorney if you are represented, will need to present to the court specific reasons why dissemination of the information should be limited.

5.8   I own my business. Will I have to disclose my business records?

Yes, you may be required to provide extensive records of your business in the discovery process. However, it is common for the court to protect the confidentiality of these records by issuing a protective order so that the business records are protected from unauthorized dissemination.

5.9   It's been two months since my lawyer sent interrogatories to my spouse, and we still don't have his answers. I answered mine on time. Is there anything that can be done to speed up the process?

The failure or refusal of a spouse to follow the rules of discovery can add to both the frustration and expense of the divorce process. Talk with your attorney about filing a *motion to compel,* seeking a court order that your spouse provides the requested information by a certain date. A request for attorney fees for the filing of the motion may also be appropriate.

Ask your lawyer whether a subpoena of information from an employer or a financial institution would be a more cost-effective way to get needed facts and documents if your spouse remains uncooperative.

5.10   What is a *deposition*?

A *deposition* is the asking and answering of questions under oath, outside of court, in the presence of a court reporter. A deposition may be taken of you, your spouse, or potential witnesses in your divorce case, including experts. Both attorneys will be present. You and your spouse also have the right to be present during the taking of depositions of any witnesses in your case. Depositions are not performed in every divorce. They are most common in cases involving contested complex financial issues and if expert witnesses are used in a case.

After your deposition is completed, the questions and answers will be transcribed, that is, typed by the court reporter exactly as given and bound into one or more volumes. You will then have an opportunity to read the transcript and make any corrections if something was incorrectly transcribed.

5.11   What is the purpose of a deposition?

A deposition can serve a number of purposes such as:

- Supporting the settlement process by providing valuable information
- Helping your attorney determine who to use as witnesses at trial
- Aiding in the assessment of a witness's credibility, that is, whether the witness appears to be telling the truth
- Helping avoid surprises at the trial by learning the testimony of witnesses in advance
- Preserving testimony in the event the witness becomes unavailable for trial

Depositions can be essential tools in a divorce, especially when a case is likely to proceed to trial.

5.12   Will what I say in my deposition be used against me when we go to court?

Usually, a deposition is used to develop trial strategy and obtain information in preparation for trial. In some circumstances, a deposition may be used at trial.

If you are called later to testify as a witness and you give testimony contrary to your deposition, your deposition can be used to impeach you by showing the inconsistency in your statements. It is important to review your deposition prior to your live testimony to ensure consistency and prepare yourself for the types of questions you may be asked.

5.13   How should I prepare for my deposition?

To prepare for your deposition, review the important documents in your case, such as the petition for dissolution, your answers to interrogatories, your affidavit of financial information, and any papers submitted for temporary orders.

Gather all documents you've been asked to provide at your deposition. Deliver them to your attorney in advance of your deposition for copying and review. Talk to your attorney about the types of questions you can expect to be asked. Discuss with him or her any questions you are concerned about answering.

5.14   What will I be asked? Can I refuse to answer questions?

Questions in a deposition can cover a broad range of topics including your education, work, income, and family. The attorney is allowed to ask anything that is reasonably calculated to lead to the discovery of admissible evidence. If the question may lead to relevant information, it can be asked in a deposition, even though it may be inadmissible at trial. Before answering any questions, skip a beat to give your attorney an opportunity to object to a question. A list of categories of questions are included in the Appendix.

Your attorney may object to inappropriate questions. If there is an objection, say nothing until the attorneys discuss the objection. You will be directed by your attorney whether to answer the question.

5.15   What if I give incorrect information in my deposition?

You will be under oath during your deposition, so it is very important that you be truthful. If you give incorrect information by mistake, contact your attorney as soon as you realize the error. If you lie during your deposition, you risk being impeached by the other lawyer during your divorce trial. This could cause you to lose credibility with the court, rendering your testimony less valuable. It is better to correct the information before trial than to wait and try to correct the information at trial.

You will also have the opportunity to read your deposition transcript. Read it carefully and make any corrections.

5.16 What if I don't know or can't remember the answer to a question?

You may be asked questions about which you have no knowledge during the deposition. It is always acceptable to say "I don't know" if you do not have the knowledge. Similarly, if you cannot remember, simply say so. It is important not to guess or to assume you understand the question being asked. If you need the attorney asking the question to clarify, you should ask them to clarify.

5.17 What else do I need to know about having my deposition taken?

The following suggestions will help you to give a successful deposition:

- Prepare for your deposition by reviewing and providing necessary documents and talking with your lawyer.
- Get a good night's sleep the night before.
- Eat something before you arrive because depositions can go for several hours.
- Arrive early for your deposition so that you have time to get comfortable with your surroundings.
- Relax. You are going to be asked questions about matters you know about. Your deposition is likely to begin with routine matters such as your education and work history.

At the deposition your lawyer will be there to protect you from answering unfair questions or questions that may call for information protected by the attorney-client privilege. In answering questions, keep the following items in mind:

- Tell the truth. The first thing the court reporter will do is to swear you in, just like the bailiff will do at the time of trial or an evidentiary hearing. Your testimony is going to have the same force and effect that it does in a court of law. Remember the best answer is not one that you guess at or infer from the question. The best answer is just the truth.

- Stay calm. Your spouse's lawyer will be judging your credibility and demeanor. Do not argue with the attorneys.

- Take your time. There is no need to rush your answer. Wait until the question has been asked and then answer the question asked. This serves several purposes. First, it ensures that you have heard the complete question and understand what is being asked. Second, it allows your attorney to hear the complete question and object to the question if necessary. Third, it allows the court reporter to take down the testimony without having to stop and ask the question and answer to be repeated.

- Listen carefully to the entire question. Do not try to anticipate questions or start thinking about your answer before the attorney has finished asking the question. You may not be answering the question that is being asked. In addition, the court reporter can only take down one person speaking at a time.

- Enunciate clearly and avoid saying "un-huh" because it is difficult to determine what that means. "Uh-huh" is difficult for the court reporter to distinguish from "unh-unh" and may result in inaccuracies in the transcript.

- Avoid shaking or nodding your head in response to the question because the court reporter can only take down audible responses not gestures.

- Answer the question directly. If the question calls only for "yes" or "no," provide such an answer.

- Do not volunteer information. Answer only what the question specifically requests. If the lawyer wants to elicit more information, he or she will do so in following questions.

- Don't guess, exaggerate, or speculate. Give the best short, truthful answer possible. If your answer is an estimate or approximation, say so. Do not let an attorney pin you down to anything you are not sure about. For example, if you cannot remember the number of times an event occurred, say that. If the attorney asks you if it was more than ten times, answer only if you can. If you can provide a range (more than ten but less than twenty) with reasonable certainty, you may do so.

- Answer questions only with what you personally know, saw, heard, or did unless the question asks you otherwise.
- If you do not know or cannot remember the answer, say so. That is an adequate answer.
- If an attorney mischaracterizes something you said earlier, say so.
- Answer all questions with words, rather than gestures or sounds.
- If an objection is made, stop answering the question and wait for further instructions. There are only a limited number of objections that can stop you from answering a question. The most important one is if the question calls for information that can only be answered by divulging something your attorney told you. Most objections will just be questions your lawyer is making as to the form of the question. Your lawyer is making the objection to preserve the right to object at the time of trial. However, you will still be instructed to answer the question. If you need a break at any point in the deposition, you have the right to request one. You can talk to your attorney during such a break.

Remember that the purpose of your deposition is to support a good outcome in your case. Completing it will help your case to move forward.

5.18   Can I bring notes to the deposition?

If you bring notes to the deposition or refer to anything during the deposition the questioner has the right to ask to see a copy. Make sure anything you bring in to the deposition and refer to is not something you mind sharing with the other side.

5.19   Will my spouse be present?

Your spouse has a right to be at the deposition. If your spouse attends, avoid eye contact with him or her. This is not the time to engage in a battle of wills or to become distracted. This is the equivalent of a court proceeding. Be professional, be in control, and stay focused.

5.20 Are depositions always necessary? Does every witness have to be deposed?

Depositions are less likely to be needed if you and your spouse are reaching agreement on most of the facts in your case and you are moving toward a settlement. They are more likely to be needed in cases where parenting time is in dispute or where there are complex financial issues. Although depositions of all witnesses are usually unnecessary, it is common to take depositions of expert witnesses.

5.21 Will I get a copy of the depositions in my case?

Ask your attorney for copies of the depositions in your case. It will be important for you to carefully review your deposition if your case proceeds to trial.

6

Mediation and
Alternative Dispute Resolution

At some point during the course of your divorce, you will likely want to consider whether there is a better way to resolve the issues between you and your spouse without going to trial. In the beginning there may be a lot of conflict between you and your spouse. You may feel the need to "win" and therefore treat every issue, every motion, every proceeding in your matter as an attempt to show your spouse that your position is correct and to beat up on the other side.

Perhaps you and your spouse are parting ways amicably. Although you are in disagreement about how your divorce should be settled, you are clear that you want the process to be respectful and without hostility. You would rather spend your hard-earned money on your children's college education than on legal fees.

In either case, going to trial and having a judge make all the decisions in your divorce is not a forgone conclusion. In fact, most divorce cases settle without the need for a trial. Mediation is a form of *alternative dispute resolution,* sometimes referred to as *ADR.* A mediation can help you and your spouse resolve your disputed issues and reach your own agreements without taking your case before the judge, who will make decisions about your life.

Resolving your divorce through a mediated settlement has many advantages. You can achieve a mutually satisfying agreement, a known outcome, little risk of appeal, and often enjoy significantly lower legal fees. Despite the circumstances that led to the end of your marriage, it might be possible for your divorce to conclude peacefully.

6.1   What is *mediation*?

Mediation is the process of by which a neutral third party helps the parties reach agreement on disputed issues. A mediator cannot give legal advice. Rather, the mediator's job is to help you and your spouse reach agreement on all the issues. Depending on the issues in your case, this includes division of property, spousal maintenance, child support, and parenting time.

After an agreement is reached, your agreement will be placed in the proper form and submitted to the court as part of a consent decree for dissolution of marriage. The court will then sign the consent decree as an order of the court in order to dissolve the marriage.

If your case does not settle during mediation, what was said in mediation and the offers exchanged in mediation are confidential. Accordingly, if your spouse makes an offer in mediation that is not accepted, you may not admit that offer in court to show that your spouse had previously taken a position different than the position taken at trial. This encourages both parties to be free to talk openly with the mediator without fear that the information conveyed will be used against you later in court.

6.2   What is *collaborative divorce*?

Collaborative divorce is alternative dispute resolution that is designed to assist parties who have a strong commitment to amicably resolving their disputes and avoiding litigation. You and your spouse each hire an attorney trained in the collaborative law process. You and your lawyers enter into an agreement which provides that in the event either you or your spouse decides to take the case to court both of you must terminate services with your collaborative lawyers and start anew.

Often spouses in the collaborative process enlist the support of other professionals, such as an independent financial advisor or coaches to support them through the process. Although the process may be lengthy, it enables the focus to shift away from the conflict and toward finding solutions. The attorneys become a part of the team supporting settlement rather than advocates adding to the conflict.

Talk to your lawyer about whether your case would be well suited to the collaborative law process.

6.3   What is a *settlement conference*?

A *settlement conference* is another way to resolve your case. It is similar to mediation, but it is set by the court usually through the alternative dispute resolution program. You, your spouse, and your lawyers will meet with a settlement conference judge or a lawyer acting as a judge *pro tem* to attempt to negotiate a settlement. In some cases, the judge assigned to your case may conduct the settlement conference. The settlement conference usually lasts two to three hours and, because it is at no cost to the parties, is a less costly way to settle disputes.

Settlement conferences are most effective when both parties and their attorneys see the potential for a negotiated resolution and have the necessary information to accomplish that goal. Accordingly, a settlement conference works best when it is close to the trial date so that discovery has been completed and both parties know the strengths and weaknesses of their case.

For the purpose of this chapter, no distinction is made between mediation and settlement conferences as the goals and end result are the same.

6.4   Can my lawyer be present for the mediation?

Depending on the type of mediation that is conducted, your lawyer may be present. There are several different ways to utilize a mediator. If lawyers are not present, the mediator will usually conduct the negotiations with both parties at the same time and in the same room. The mediator's job is not to give legal advice, but to help the parties reach their own agreement. The mediator will help the parties explore different options and arrive at a settlement on each issue.

Mediation may also take place with lawyers present. In such cases your lawyer and you are usually in one room, while your spouse and your spouse's lawyer are in a different room. The mediator will then go back and forth between the rooms attempting to negotiate a settlement. This method works particularly well because your lawyer will be there to give you legal advice and can advise on the risks and benefits of accepting a particular proposal offered by your spouse. At the same time, you do not have to be in the same room as your spouse, which may help to facilitate a more open exchange of information and ideas that can be conveyed through the mediator.

6.5   My lawyer said that mediation can reduce delays in completing my divorce. How can they do this?

When the issues in your divorce are decided by a judge instead of by you and your spouse, there are many opportunities for delay. These can include:

- Waiting for the trial date

- Having to reschedule the trial if there is a conflict in the calendar of the attorneys, the parties, or a necessary witness

- Waiting for the judge's ruling on your case

- Needing additional court hearings after your trial to resolve disputes about the intention of your judge's rulings, issues that were overlooked, or disagreement regarding the language of the decree

Each one of these events holds the possibility of delaying your divorce by days, weeks, or even months. Mediating the terms of your divorce decree can eliminate these delays and provide certainty.

6.6   How can mediation lower the costs of my divorce?

If your case is not settled by agreement, you will be going to trial. If the issues in your case are many or if they are complex, such as spousal support or parenting time, the attorney's fees and other costs of going to trial can be tremendous.

By settling your case without going to trial, you may be able to save thousands of dollars in legal fees. Preparing for trial involves a number of steps including preparing pretrial statements, preparing direct and cross-examination of each of the witnesses, and assembling and organizing all your exhibits, in addition to spending time in court. By settling your case you will avoid not only these fees and costs but also fees and costs in any posttrial motions or appeals.

6.7   Are there other benefits to mediating a settlement?

Yes. A divorce resolved by a mediated agreement can have these additional benefits:

Recognizing common goals. Mediation allows for brainstorming between the parties and lawyers. Looking at all possible solutions, even the impractical ones, invites creative solutions to common goals. For example, suppose you and your spouse both agree that you need to pay your spouse some amount of equity for the family home you will keep, but you have no cash to make the payment. At trial the court is limited in either requiring a payment for equity in the home or selling the home if you cannot pay. However, in mediation you might come up with a number of options for accomplishing your goal such as a payment plan or exchanging some property in exchange for equity in the home. Mediation allows you to choose the best option for your family.

Addressing the unique circumstances of your situation. Settlements reached by agreement allow you and your spouse to consider the unique circumstances of your situation in formulating a good outcome. For example, suppose you disagree about the parenting times for the Thanksgiving holiday. The judge might order you to alternate the holiday each year, even though you both would have preferred to have your child share the day.

Creating a safe place for communication. Mediation gives each party an opportunity to be heard. Perhaps you and your spouse have not yet had an opportunity to share directly your concerns about settlement. For example, you might be worried about how the temporary parenting time arrangement is impacting your children, but have not yet talked to your spouse about it. A mediation session or settlement conference can be a safe place for you and your spouse to communicate your concerns about your children or your finances through the third-party mediator.

Fulfilling your children's needs. You may see that your children would be better served by you and your spouse deciding their future rather than by a judge who does not know, love, and understand your children like the two of you do.

Eliminating the risk and uncertainty of trial. If a judge decides the outcome of your divorce, you give up control over the terms of the settlement. The decisions are left in the hands of the judge. If you and your spouse reach agreement, however, you have the power to eliminate the risk of an uncertain outcome.

Reducing the risk of harm to your children. If your case goes to trial, it is likely that you and your spouse will give testimony that will be upsetting to each other. As the conflict increases, the relationship between you and your spouse inevitably deteriorates. This can be harmful to your children. Contrast this with mediation, in which you open your communication and seek to reach agreement. It is not unusual for the relationship between the parents to improve as the professionals create a safe environment for rebuilding communication and reaching agreements in the best interest of a child.

Having the support of professionals. Using trained professionals, such as mediators and lawyers, to support you can help you to reach a settlement that you might think is impossible. These professionals have skills to help you focus on what is most important to you and shift your attention away from irrelevant facts. They understand the law and know the possible outcomes if your case goes to trial.

Lowering stress. The process of preparing for and going to court can be stressful. Your energy is also going toward caring for your children, looking at your finances, and coping with the emotions of divorce. You might decide that you would be better served by settling your case rather than proceeding to trial.

Achieving closure. When you are going through a divorce, the process can feel as though it is taking an eternity. By reaching agreement, you and your spouse are better able to put the divorce behind you and move forward with your lives.

6.8   Is mediation mandatory?

Not necessarily. Although mediation is not mandatory in dissolution of marriage actions, some form of alternative dispute resolution is usually required, or at least expected by the trial judge, in most cases. However, if this is a post-decree matter, meaning you are already divorced and you now have an issue that has arisen regarding the children, such as a request by one party to change the parenting plan, there is generally a provision in your previous parenting plan agreement that requires you to attempt mediation prior to filing an action in court. However, talk to your attorney to see if mediation is a requirement in your post-decree case.

6.9 My spouse abused me and I am afraid to participate in mediation. Should I participate anyway?

If you have been a victim of domestic violence by your spouse, it is important that you discuss the appropriateness of mediation with your attorney. Mediation may not be a safe way for you to reach agreement.

Prior to allowing mediation to proceed, the mediator will ask you whether you have been a victim of domestic violence. This is critical for the mediator to both assess your safety and to ensure that the balance of power in the mediation process is maintained.

Talk with your attorney if you have experienced domestic violence or if you feel threatened or intimidated by your spouse. If so, your case may be referred to an approved specialized mediator for parents involved in high conflict situations. It may be possible to mediate with you and your spouse in different rooms or during separate sessions.

If you feel threatened or intimidated by your spouse, talk to your attorney to ensure that you and your spouse arrive at different times for the mediation and that you are kept entirely in separate rooms. You may also request to have the mediation occur at your lawyer's office, where you feel more comfortable.

6.10 What training and credentials do mediators have?

The background of mediators varies. Some are attorneys; many come from other backgrounds such as counseling. If the court assigns a mediator through the alternative dispute resolution process, the mediators are individuals who have filled out an application and have been determined to be qualified to conduct settlement conferences in family law matters. If you are choosing a private mediator, your attorney will have a list of qualified mediators who they have worked with in the past and can help choose a mediator who would be right for your particular case.

6.11   What types of issues can be mediated?

All of the issues in your case can be mediated. The issues for mediation include property division, spousal maintenance, child support, legal decision-making, and parenting time. It is important prior to walking into a mediation to discuss with your lawyer your goals, strategy for the mediation, and the issues you would like to resolve. It is equally important that you understand your best and worst case senarios if you went to court. You certainly would not want to settle in mediation for something that is worse than what you would obtain if you went to trial. You may decide that certain issues are nonnegotiable for you. Discuss this with your attorney in advance of any mediation session so that he or she can help focus the discussion in mediation on the issues you are open to looking at.

6.12   What is the role of my attorney in the mediation process?

The role of your attorney in the mediation process will vary. In some cases, parties attend mediation without attorneys and try to work out a resolution between themselves with the assistance of the mediator. In other cases, you may still attend the mediation without your attorney, but you may want your attorney to be available by telephone or to be available to come to the mediation at some point.

Other types of mediation will involve the attorneys in the entire process. Typically, you and your attorney will be in one room and your spouse and his or her attorney in a different room. The mediator will then go back and forth between the two rooms attempting to arrive at a settlement. In this setting your attorney is able to give you advice during the mediation and help you explore the risks and benefits of accepting a particular settlement offer. The attorney may also help raise issues that you may not have thought about on your own, such as the tax consequences of certain offers or the possibility of modifying the terms in the future.

6.13   How do I prepare for mediation?

Prior to attending a mediation session with your spouse, discuss with your attorney the issues you intend to mediate. In particular, be sure to discuss spousal support, property division, child support, legal decision-making, and parenting time arrangements for minor children. Enlist your attorney's support in identifying your intentions for the mediation. Make a list of the issues important to you. For example, when it comes to your child, you might consider whether it is your child's safety, the parenting time schedule, or the ability to attend your children's events that concerns you most.

When spousal maintenance is an issue, discuss with your attorney a range of possible amounts and the possible duration. Determine whether the amounts will be taxable income, nonmodifiable, or subject to other limitations. In mediation you have the ability to alter the terms that would otherwise apply under the law, and therefore have greater flexibility in negotiating a settlement.

Be forward looking. Giving thought to your desired outcomes while approaching mediation with an open mind and heart is the best way to move closer to settlement.

6.14   Do children attend the mediation sessions?

No. Just as with court, children will not attend the mediation.

If you think your child is of sufficient age and maturity to give input as to the parenting time schedule they would like (generally children who are teenagers), ask your lawyer about the possibility of having your child interviewed or having your child represented by their own attorney. Although the court will need to order that the child be interviewed or that an attorney be allowed to represent the child's interest, these may be some of the options available prior to a mediation to obtain input from your child.

In some cases where the court does not believe a child is of sufficient age and maturity to have their own attorney, the court may order that a best interest attorney be appointed in order to give input as to what would be in the best interest of the child for purposes of parenting time or legal decision-making. Due to the costs involved in paying for either a best interest attorney or child's attorney, the situations where a child has his or her own representation or a best interest attorney is appointed are rare.

6.15   What should I take to the mediation?

Being well prepared for the mediation can help you make the most of this opportunity to resolve your case without the need to go to trial. Actions you should take and provide to your attorney in advance of the mediation include:

* Gather all necessary information for your attorney regarding your finances. This includes current pay stub, tax returns, W-2's, debt amounts (current mortgage statements, credit card statement for six months prior to the petition for dissolution through the current time), current bank records, pension and retirement plan balances, and asset values (such as home appraisals and values of the vehicles). If child support is an issue provide your lawyer with the information on the cost to insure the children for health insurance, as well as any costs incurred for child care, private school, and extracurricular activities.

* Fill out an *affidavit of financial information* provided by your attorney. The affidavit of financial information attempts to capture the expenses you will have after the divorce to determine what you need for spousal maintenance if you are asking for spousal maintenance or what you can afford to pay for spousal maintenance if your spouse is requesting support.

* If you need health insurance after the divorce because you are currently covered by your spouse's insurance, check with an insurance agent to determine the cost of insurance and if you are currently under medical care whether your current doctors are covered by the new insurance you intend to obtain.

* If you and your spouse have life insurance, provide copies of any statements showing the type of insurance you have and the cash surrender value if any.

* Prepare an inventory list of all items of personal property, including furniture, furnishings, antiques, artwork, jewelry, and similar items together with your estimate of current value. Remember used furniture is usually not worth very much so do not use the price

you paid for the item but the price you would be able to sell the item for in its current condition.

- Identify all vehicles, recreational vehicles, motorcycles, boats, and ATVs and approximate value based on the condition of each vehicle. You can find values at (www.kbb.com). Prepare a list of topics of concern. Your lawyer can assist you in understanding your rights under the law so that you can have realistic expectations for the outcome of negotiations.
- Bring a positive attitude, a listening ear, and an open mind. Come with the attitude that your case will settle. Be willing to listen to the information provided by the mediator, and then to share your position. Resist the urge to interpret everything in a negative light.

Few cases settle without each side demonstrating flexibility and a willingness to compromise. Most cases settle when the parties are able to bring these qualities to the process.

6.16 I want my attorney to look over the agreements my spouse and I discussed in mediation before I give my final approval. Is this possible?

Yes. If your attorney is not present in the mediation or does not participate in the mediation, you still should not sign anything without your attorney's review. Accordingly, before giving your written or final approval to any agreements reached in mediation, it is critical that your attorney review the agreements first. This is necessary to ensure that you understand the terms of the settlement and its implications. Your attorney will also review the agreement for compliance with Arizona law.

6.17 Who pays for mediation?

The cost of private mediation must be paid for by you or your spouse. Often it is a shared expense. Expect your mediator to address the matter of fees before your mediation. The mediator may request a retainer for a certain number of hours in advance.

Settlement conferences as discussed in question 6.3 are set by the court and are conducted by a settlement conference judge or judge *pro tem* and do not charge a separate fee.

6.18   What if mediation fails?

If mediation is not successful, you still may be able to settle your case through negotiations between the attorneys. Also, you and your spouse can agree to preserve the settlements that were reached and to take only the remaining disputed issues to the judge for trial. The agreements that are reached are written up and signed by the parties. After this is done it is a binding agreement between you and your spouse on the issues that have been settled.

6.19   Why should I consider mediation or a settlement conference when the attorneys can negotiate through letters and phone calls?

Sometimes it is helpful to have a neutral third party involved in mediating a case. A skilled mediator can often help the parties see different perspectives and the risk and benefits of going to trial. In addition, oftentimes information is able to be immediately provided, which expedites the process versus the delays that often occur when negotiation takes place through correspondence and calls between the attorneys.

6.20   How long will mediation take?

Depending on the number of issues involved and the complexity of the issues mediation may last only a couple of hours or may last all day. An effort is made to confirm which issues are resolved and which issues remain disputed. Then one by one the issues are addressed.

6.21   What happens if my spouse and I settled some but not all of the issues in our divorce?

You and your spouse can agree to maintain the agreements you have reached and let the judge decide those matters that you are unable to resolve. If you indicate you will settle some of the issues, you will be asked to sign a written document confirming the terms of the agreement reached. This is called a *Rule 69 Agreement* and binds the parties to the terms agreed to in the settlement. Although there may be other terms that will need to be added, you cannot change the terms of the agreement that were settled upon.

6.22 What if I feel pressure to settle and I do not think the settlement is in my best interest?

No one will force you to settle. The settlement is entirely up to you. You must ultimately be happy with the settlement and wanting to put the matter behind you. Oftentimes, people have regrets the next day and think that they may have been better off going to trial. If you think that you will have any regrets over the settlement, DON'T SETTLE. After you settle it is very difficult to change the terms of the settlement.

Settling is an important decision. You are giving up rights to a trial and a decision by a judge by settling. The reason most people settle is to avoid the uncertainty of trial and the emotional aspects of litigating a personal family matter in court. In court there are winners and losers. Trial is always a risk. The only certainty is settlement, which is why many people choose that route.

6.23 If my spouse and I reach an agreement, how long will it take before it can be finalized?

If a settlement is reached one of the attorneys will draft a *consent decree* for signature by you and your spouse. As soon as the consent decree is signed by you and your spouse, and so long as the sixty-day waiting period has expired, it will be submitted to the judge for approval and is usually finalized in several business days.

7

Emergency: When You Fear Your Spouse

Going through a divorce can be difficult emotionally as well as frightening at times. Maybe your spouse has threatened to take the children away from you or has emptied the bank accounts. In some cases, there may have even been physical abuse or threats of abuse, which you fear may escalate as a result of the divorce process.

Facing an emergency situation in divorce can feel as though your entire life has been turned upside down. You may not be able to concentrate on anything else. At the same time, you may be paralyzed with anxiety and have no idea how to begin to protect yourself. Remember that you have overcome many challenges in your life before this moment. There are people willing to help you. You have strength and wisdom you may not yet even realize. Step by step, you will make it through this time.

When facing an emergency, do your best to focus on what to do in the immediate moment. Set aside your worries about the future for another day. Now it is time to stay in the present moment, let others support you, and start taking action right away. Your lawyer is there to help you with the options and to seek emergency relief on your behalf.

7.1 My spouse has deserted me, and I need to get divorced as quickly as possible. What is my first step?

Your first step is to seek legal advice at your earliest opportunity. The earlier you get legal counsel to advise you about your rights, the better. The initial consultation will answer most of your questions and start you on an action plan for getting your divorce underway.

7.2   I am afraid if I file for divorce my spouse will empty all the bank accounts or flee the state with the children. What can I do to stop that from happening?

Upon filing of the petition for dissolution a preliminary injunction is issued; the injunction is effective for you immediately on service and for your spouse upon service of the petition. The *preliminary injunction* prohibits a number of actions by either spouse during the pendency of the case. These actions include:

- You may not hide earnings or community property from your spouse.

- You may not take out a loan on the community property.

- You may not sell the community property or give it away to someone, unless you have the written permission of your spouse or written permission from the court. The law allows for situations in which you may need to transfer joint or community property as part of the everyday running of a business or if the sale of community property is necessary to meet necessities of life, such as food, shelter, or clothing, or court fees and attorney fees associated with this action.

- You may not harass or bother your spouse or the children.

- You may not physically abuse or threaten your spouse or the children,

- You may not take the minor children, common to your marriage, out of the state of Arizona for any reasons without a written agreement between you and your spouse or a court order.

- You may not remove or cause to be removed the other party or the minor children of the parties from any existing insurance coverage, including medical, hospital, dental, automobile, and disability insurance. All insurance coverage must remain in full force and effect.

7.3 I'm afraid my abusive spouse will try to hurt me or our children if I say I want a divorce. What can I do legally to protect myself and my children?

If you are in an abusive relationship it is important to develop a plan for the safety of you and the children. Although often people feel ashamed or embarrassed to admit they are in an abusive relationship, it is important that you discuss this with your attorney at your first meeting. Your risk of harm from an abusive spouse increases when you leave. For this reason, all actions must be taken with safety as the first concern.

Find a lawyer who understands domestic violence. Talk to your lawyer about the concerns for your safety and that of your children. Ask your lawyer about obtaining an *order of protection*. This is a court order that may offer a number of protections including not only staying away from you, but staying away from the residence where you and the children are residing, your place of employment, and places that you attend such as the children's school, church, or synagogue.

7.4 I am afraid to meet with a lawyer because I am terrified my spouse will find out and get violent. What should I do?

Schedule an initial consultation with an attorney who is experienced in working with domestic violence victims. When you schedule the appointment, let the firm know your situation and instruct the law office not to place any calls to you which you think your spouse might discover. If possible, pay for your consultation in cash.

In addition to advising the law firm not to contact you by telephone at a number your spouse might discover, also avoid corresponding by e-mail unless your e-mail and password are secure. If your spouse has access to your e-mail account, set up a different account and change your password before communicating by e-mail with your lawyer.

Consultations with your attorney are confidential. Your lawyer has an ethical duty to not disclose your meeting with anyone outside of the law firm. Let your attorney know your concerns so that extra precautions can be taken by the law office in handling your file.

7.5   I want to give my attorney all the information needed so my children and I are safe from my spouse. What does this include?

Provide your attorney with complete information about the history, background, nature, and evidence of your abuse including:

- The types of abuse (for example, physical, sexual, verbal, financial, mental, emotional)
- The dates, time frames, or occasions
- The locations
- Whether you were ever treated medically
- Any police reports made
- E-mails, letters, notes, or journal entries
- Any photographs taken
- Any witnesses to the abuse or evidence of the abuse
- Any statements made by your spouse admitting the abuse
- Alcohol or drug abuse
- The presence of guns or other weapons

The more the information you provide to your lawyer, the easier it will be for him or her to make a strong case for the protection of you and your children.

7.6   I'm not ready to hire a lawyer for a divorce, but I am afraid my spouse is going to get violent with my children and me in the meantime. What can I do?

Talk to your attorney about obtaining an order of protection if you are concerned about your safety, your children's safety, or if there has been a history of domestic abuse. If your spouse has attempted to cause you bodily injury, has caused you bodily injury, or has threatened to cause you bodily injury, you may qualify for an order of protection.

You may seek an order of protection without filing an action for divorce. An order of protection may be granted to prevent a person from engaging in certain conduct. This may include giving you exclusive possession of the family residence, restraining your spouse from contacting you, or coming near the residence, your place of employment, or your school.

The order of protection may also prohibit your spouse from possessing or purchasing a firearm or ammunition.

7.7   How do I apply for an order of protection?

Orders of protection may be obtained from judicial, municipal, and superior courts. The self-service centers at the court will have the forms to file a petition for an order of protection. Although court personnel may not give legal advice, they are available to assist in answering questions on how to fill out the forms and to provide information on the procedure.

You may also seek the advice of an attorney who has experience in domestic violence. Your attorney can help guide you through the process.

7.8   What do I have to prove to obtain an order of protection?

There are two primary conditions that must be met to obtain an order of protection. First, there must be a special relationship between the parties. This relationship includes individuals who:

- are married now or in the past
- live together now or in the past
- have a child in common
- one party is pregnant by the other party
- is a relative to the other party (brother, sister, grandparent)
- have a current or past sexual relationship

The second condition is there must have already been an act of domestic violence or reasonable cause to believe an act of domestic violence will occur. Domestic violence includes many behaviors that do not involved physical abuse and may include actions such as criminal damage to property, custodial interference, disorderly conduct, reckless display of dangerous instruments, threats, and acts of intimidation.

7.9   What's the difference between an order of protection and an injunction against harassment?

An order of protection requires that there be a special relationship between the parties as presented in question

7.8. An injunction against harassment does not require a special relationship.

To obtain an injunction against harassment a party must show that the defendant committed an act of harassment during the year prior to filing a request for an injunction or that great or irreparable harm to the person may happen in the future.

Similar to the order of protection, if an injunction against harassment is issued the court may prohibit certain activities by the defendant. These activities include prohibiting the defendant from contacting the plaintiff or going near the plaintiff's residence, place of employment, or school.

7.10 My spouse has never been violent, but I know she is going to be really angry and upset when the divorce papers are served. Do I need a protection order?

The facts of your case may not warrant an order of protection. However, the preliminary injunction that is filed at the time the petition for dissolution of marriage is filed will direct your spouse to not annoy, threaten, intimidate, or harass you while the divorce is in progress. If your spouse violates this preliminary injunction, your attorney can advise the court of the violation so that appropriate action can be taken to prohibit future violations.

7.11 I'm afraid my spouse is going to take all of the money out of the bank accounts and leave me with nothing. What can I do?

Talk to your attorney immediately. If you are worried about your spouse emptying financial accounts or selling marital assets, it is critical that you take action at once. Your attorney can advise you on your right to take possession of certain assets in order to protect them from being hidden or spent by your spouse.

Ask your lawyer about seeking a *temporary restraining order (TRO)*. There already is a preliminary injunction in place that forbids your spouse from selling, transferring, hiding, or otherwise disposing of marital property until the divorce is complete. However, a temporary restraining order may go a step further and freeze bank accounts, or transfer accounts to you or to an escrow holder for safekeeping.

A temporary restraining order is intended to prevent assets from "disappearing" before a final division of the property from your marriage is complete. If this is a concern, talk to your lawyer about the benefits of obtaining a temporary restraining order as to property prior to giving your spouse notice that you are filing for divorce.

7.12 My spouse says that I am crazy, that I am a liar, and that no judge will ever believe me if I tell the truth about the abusive behavior. What can I do if I don't have any proof?

Most domestic violence is not witnessed by third parties. Often there is little physical evidence. Even without physical evidence, a judge can enter orders to protect you and your children if you give truthful testimony about your abuse that the judge finds believable. Your own testimony of your abuse is evidence.

It is very common for persons who abuse others to claim that their victims are liars and to make statements intended to discourage disclosure of the abuse. This is yet another form of controlling behavior.

Your attorney's skills and experience will support you to give effective testimony in the courtroom to establish your case. Let your lawyer know your concerns so that a strong case can be presented to the judge based upon your persuasive statements of the truth of your experience.

7.13 My spouse told me that if I ever file for divorce, I'll never see my child again. Should I be worried about my child being abducted?

Your fear that your spouse will abduct your child is a common one. It can be helpful to look at some of the factors that appear to increase the risk that your child will be removed from the state by the other parent.

Most abductions are made by men. They are often from marriages that cross culture, race, religion, or ethnicity. A lower socioeconomic status, prior criminal record, and limited social or economic ties to the community can also increase risk.

Programming and brainwashing are almost always present in cases where a child is at risk for being kidnapped by a parent, and efforts to isolate the child may also be seen. Exit activities such as obtaining a new passport, getting financial matters in order, or contacting a moving company could be indicators.

Talk to your lawyer to assess the risks in your particular case. Together you can determine whether statements by your spouse are threats intended to control or intimidate you or whether legal action is needed to protect your child.

7.14 What legal steps can be taken to prevent my spouse from removing our child from the state?

If you are concerned about your child being removed from the state, ask your lawyer whether any of these options might be available in your case:

- A court order prohibiting your spouse from having parenting time with the child until a hearing can be held
- A court order directing your spouse to turn over passports for the child and your spouse to the court
- The posting of a bond prior to your spouse exercising parenting time
- Supervised visitation

Both state and federal laws are designed to provide protection from the removal of children from one state to another when a custody matter is brought and to protect children from kidnapping. *The Uniform Child Custody Jurisdiction Enforcement Act (UCCJEA)* was passed to encourage the custody of children to be decided in the state where they have been living most recently and where they have the most ties. *The Parental Kidnapping Prevention Act (PKPA)* makes it a federal crime for a parent to kidnap a child in violation of a valid custody order.

If you are concerned about your child being abducted, talk with your lawyer about all options available to you for your child's protection.

7.15 How quickly can I get a divorce in Arizona?

There are a number of time requirements for obtaining a divorce in Arizona. Either you or your spouse must have been domiciled in the state for at least ninety days prior to the filing of the petition for dissolution of marriage. After you file your divorce, your spouse must be given notice of the divorce.

A sixty-day waiting period is required for every Arizona divorce. This period begins on either the date a process server or the sheriff hand delivers the petition for dissolution to you or your spouse or the date that a voluntary appearance signed by the responding party is filed with the court.

A decree of dissolution of marriage cannot be entered until the sixty-day waiting period has expired, although most cases do not resolve this quickly. The length of time it takes to resolve your case or to go to trial depends in large part upon the extent to which you and your spouse reach agreement on the issues without the necessity of trial, the court where your action is pending, and the judge's caseload.

Your divorce becomes final after the judge signs the decree of dissolution of marriage and it is filed with the clerk of the court. You are free to marry after the divorce becomes final.

7.16 I really need a divorce quickly. Will the divorce I get in another state be valid in Arizona?

This depends. It will be valid if you are able to meet the jurisdictional requirements in the other state in order to obtain a divorce. That means you must meet that state or country's residency requirements and waiting period. In addition, the other state or country must have jurisdiction over your spouse, the marital assets, and the children in order to enter orders that will be recognized in Arizona.

If you are domiciled in Arizona, your marital assets are in Arizona, and the children reside with you in Arizona it is much better to simply go through the process of obtaining an Arizona divorce. Otherwise, you may find that you spent a lot of time and money on obtaining a "quickie" divorce that is not going to be recognized in Arizona.

7.17 If either my spouse or I file for divorce, will I be ordered out of my home? Who decides who gets to live in the house while we go through the divorce?

Neither party is required to leave the marital residence during the divorce unless a court orders one party to leave.

If you and your spouse cannot reach an agreement regarding which of you will leave the residence during the divorce, you may seek a temporary order for exclusive possession of the home until the case is concluded.

The judge will only grant your temporary order for exclusive possession of the home under certain conditions. You must be able to show that physical or emotional harm may result if it is not granted. Abusive behavior is one basis for seeking temporary possession of the home. In addition, talk to your attorney about other factors that may be relevant.

Other factors that may be important in determining who stays in the home include:

- Whether one of you owned the home prior to the marriage
- After provisions are made for payment of temporary support, who can afford to remain in the home or obtain other housing
- Who is most likely to be awarded the home in the divorce
- Options available to each of you for other temporary housing, including other homes or family members who live in the area
- Special needs that would make a move unduly burdensome, such as a health condition
- Self-employment from home, which could not be readily moved, such as a child-care business

8

Legal Decision-Making and Parenting Time

The term *legal decision-making* refers to the right and responsibility of a parent to make nonemergency decisions involving the child. These decisions include education, health care, religious training and personal care. *Parenting time* refers to the schedule of time that each parent has with the child. Each parent is responsible during their parenting time to provide the child with food, clothing, and shelter and to make routine decisions concerning the care of the child.

Ever since you and your spouse began talking about divorce, chances are your children have been your greatest concern. You or your spouse might have postponed the decision to seek divorce because of concern about the impact on your children. Now that the time has come, you might still have doubts about whether your children will be alright after the divorce.

Remember that you have been making wise and loving decisions for your children since they were born. You have always done your best to see that they had everything they really needed. You loved them and protected them. This will not change because you are going through your divorce. You were a good parent before the divorce and you will be a good parent after the divorce.

It can be difficult not to worry about how the sharing of parenting time with your spouse will affect your children. You may also have fears about whether your spouse will try to alienate you from your children's lives.

The court's focus in determining decision-making and parenting time is going to be based on the best interest of the children. Absent circumstances making it not in the best interest of the minor children to have substantial parenting time with each parent it is likely that the court order will not only give you a lot of time with your children but also a generous opportunity to be involved in their day-to-day lives.

With the help of your lawyer, you can make sound decisions regarding the parenting time arrangement that is in the best interest of your children.

8.1 What types of custody are awarded in Arizona?

Arizona does not use the word "custody" in making decisions about a minor child. Effective January 1, 2013, the legislature eliminated the word *custody* from the statutes. Instead, Arizona uses the terms *legal decision-making* and *parenting time* to better define what a court must do in deciding issues related to a minor child.

8.2 Will the court award me or my spouse the right to make all decisions?

The court will award either sole legal decision-making or joint legal decision-making. *Sole legal decision-making* gives one parent the right to make all major decisions for the child, without having to consult with the other parent.

Joint legal decision-making requires the parties to share decision-making responsibilities. Neither parent's rights are superior to the other parent's rights, except on specific issues as set forth by the court.

Arizona provides by statute that, absent contrary evidence, it is in the best interest of the child that both parents participate in decision-making about the child. Discuss with your lawyer whether there is any evidence to support the following factors to be considered by the court:

- The agreement or lack of agreement by the parties as to joint legal decision-making
- Whether a lack of agreement is unreasonable or influenced by a reason not related to the child's best interest

- The past, present, and future ability of the parents to cooperate in decision-making
- Whether joint legal decision-making is logistically possible

8.3 How will the court determine the parenting time for the minor child?

It is the policy of the state of Arizona that, absent contrary evidence, the child should have "substantial, frequent, meaningful and continuing parenting time with both parents." The court will always look to the best interest of the child in determining a parenting time schedule.

8.4 What factors does the court consider in determining the best interest of the child.

The judge considers many factors in determining the best interest of the child. The court will look at all of the following factors:

Relationship between the parent and child. The past, present, and future relationship between the child and each parent is considered. This includes the nature of the bond between the parent and child and the feelings shared between the child and each parent. The court may also consider whether you or your spouse have been the primary caregiver of the minor child.

The interaction and interrelationship between the child and other persons. The interaction and interrelationship between the child and each parent as well as the child's siblings and any other person who may significantly affect the child's best interest is considered.

The child's adjustment to home, school, and community. This refers to the respective environments offered by you and your spouse. The court may consider factors such as the safety, stability, and nurturing found in each home.

The wishes of the child as to legal decision-making and parenting time. If the child is of suitable age and maturity, the child may be able to express their wishes as to legal decision-making and parenting time. This can be expressed either through the respective parents, or sometimes by the child providing information to a court appointed advisor, or by the court. However, this is only one factor and is not determinative. Arizona does not allow a child to choose the parent he or she wishes to live with. Typically, the older the child is the greater the weight the court will give to the child's preference.

The mental and physical health of all individuals involved. Arizona no longer ascribes to the "tender years" doctrine, which formerly gave a preference for custody of very young children to the mother. If one of the parents has an illness that may impair the ability to parent, it may be considered by the court. Similarly, the judge may look at special health needs of a child.

Which parent is more likely to allow frequent, meaningful, and continuing contact with the other parent. This factor might be applied in your case if there is evidence that if your spouse will not comply with the court orders or if there is evidence that your spouse may attempt to align the child with them and alienate you from your child.

Whether one parent intentionally misled the court. This factor may apply if one parent intentionally misleads the court to cause unnecessary delay, increase the costs of litigation, or tries to persuade the court to grant them legal decision-making or parenting time. Things such as asking for custody evaluations when there is no evidence to warrant an evaluation or raising allegations against the other parent that are false, may affect this factor.

Whether there has been domestic violence or child abuse. If there has been significant domestic violence, or a significant history of domestic violence, the court will not award joint legal decision-making. Domestic violence is also an important factor in determining parenting time and protection from abuse during the transfer of your child to the other parent. If domestic violence is a concern in your case, be sure to discuss it in detail with your attorney during the initial consultation so that every measure can be taken to protect the safety of you and your children.

The nature and extent of coercion or duress used by one parent in obtaining an agreement regarding legal decision-making or parenting time. The court may consider whether your spouse offered to pay you more money if you gave more parenting time, or whether you offered to accept less money in exchange for more parenting time. This type of economic coercion is not permitted in determining the best interest of the minor child.

Completion of the parenting information program. Each parent must complete an educational program that educates parents on the impact of divorce on adults and children. The superior court in your county will have a list of available programs. In some counties the program may be offered in person and online.

False reports of child abuse. Reporting a false case of child abuse against the other parent is a factor the court will consider in determining decision-making and parenting time.

When making a final determination the judge will have to make specific findings with respect to each factor. Accordingly, it is important to discuss each of the above factors in detail with your lawyer.

8.5 What's the difference between *visitation* and *parenting time*?

Historically, time spent with the noncustodial parent was referred to as *visitation*. Today, the term *parenting time* is used to refer to the time a child spends with either parent.

This change in language reflects the intention that children spend time with both parents and have two homes, as opposed to their living with one parent and visiting the other.

8.6 How can I make sure I will get to keep the children during the divorce proceedings?

You cannot ensure that your children will stay with you during the divorce process. However, the best way to provide clarity about the living arrangements and respective parenting time with your children during your divorce is to obtain a temporary order. Informal agreements between parties cannot always be trusted. Additionally, informal agreements with your spouse lack the ability to be enforced by the court. Thus, even if you and your spouse have agreed to temporary arrangements, talk with your attorney about whether this agreement should be formalized in a court order.

Obtaining a temporary order can be an important protection not only for the parenting time of your children, but also for other issues such as support, temporary exclusive possession of the marital home, temporary protection from your spouse, or attorney's fees.

Until a temporary order is entered, it's best that you continue to reside with your children. If you are considering leaving your home, talk with your attorney before making any significant changes to your living situation. If you must leave your home, take your children with you and talk with your attorney at your earliest opportunity.

8.7   I heard that a child over the age of thirteen may decide who they want to live with?

Some states allow children of a certain age to decide who they wish to live with. Arizona does not allow for a child to make the decision, regardless of the child's age. Accordingly, until the child turns eighteen, absent agreement of the parties, the court will make the decision on parenting time regardless of the age of the child.

8. 8   How much weight does a child's preference carry?

The preference of your child is only one of many factors a judge may consider in determining a parenting time schedule. The age of your child and his or her ability to express the underlying reason for their preference to live with either parent will determine the amount of weight the judge will give to your child's preference. Although there is no age at which your child's preference determines parenting time, most judges give more weight to the wishes of an older child such as a child who is sixteen or seventeen.

The reasoning underlying your child's preference is also a factor to consider. Consider the fifteen-year-old who wants to live with the mother because "Mom lets me stay out past curfew, I get a bigger allowance, and I don't have to do chores." Greater weight might be given to the preference of an eight-year-old who wants to live with mother because "she helps me with my homework, reads me bedtime stories, and doesn't call me names like Dad does."

If you see that your child's preference may be a factor in the determination of parenting time, discuss it with your lawyer so that this consideration is a part of assessing the action to be taken in your case.

8.9 How can I prove that I was the primary care provider?

One tool to assist you and your attorney in establishing your case as a primary care provider is a chart indicating the care you and your spouse have each provided for your child. The clearer you are about the history of parenting, the better job your attorney can do in presenting your case to the judge.

Look at the activities in the chart to help you review the role of you and your spouse as care providers for your child.

Parental Roles Chart

Activity	Parent 1	Parent 2
Attended prenatal medical visits		
Attended prenatal class		
Took time off work after child born		
Got up with child for feedings		
Got up with child when sick at night		
Bathed child		
Put child to sleep		
Potty-trained child		
Prepared and fed meals to child		
Helped child learn numbers, letters, colors		
Helped child with practice for music, dance lessons, sports		
Took time off work for child's appointments		
Took child to doctor visits		
Stayed home from work with sick child		
Went to pharmacy for child's medication		
Administered child's medication		
Took child to therapy		
Took child to optometrist		
Took child to dentist		
Took child to get haircuts		

Parental Roles Chart (Continued)

Activity	Parent 1	Parent 2
Bought clothing for child		
Bought school supplies for child		
Transported child to school		
Picked up child after school		
Drove carpool for child's school		
Went to child's school activities		
Helped child with homework and projects		
Attended parent-teacher conferences		
Helped in child's classroom		
Chaperoned child's school trips and activities		
Transported child to day care		
Communicated with day care providers		
Transported child from day care		
Attended day care activities		
Signed child up for sports, dance, music		
Bought equipment for sports, dance, music		
Transported child to sports, dance, music		
Attended sports, dance, music practices, dance recitals		
Coached child's sports		
Transported child from sports, dance, music		
Know child's friends and friends' families		
Took child to religious education		
Participated in child's religious education		
Obtained information and training about special needs of child		

Parental Roles Chart (Continued)

Activity	Parent 1	Parent 2
Comforted child during times of emotional upset		

Showing that you were the primary caregiver is just one factor the court considers. Even if your spouse was not a very involved parent prior to the divorce, this generally is not the sole factor the court will consider. Most judges will assume that even an uninvolved parent prior to the divorce will assume a more active role with the children after the divorce.

8.10 Do I have to let my spouse see the children before we are actually divorced?

Unless your children are at risk for being harmed by your spouse, your children should maintain regular contact with the other parent.

It is important for children to experience the presence of both parents in their lives, regardless of the separation of the parents. Even if there is no temporary order for parenting time, cooperate with your spouse in making reasonable arrangements for time with your children.

When safety is not an issue, if you deny contact with the other parent prior to trial, your judge is likely to question whether you have the best interest of your child at heart. Talk to your spouse or your lawyer about what parenting time schedule would be best for your children on a temporary basis.

8.11 I am seeing a therapist. Will that hurt my chances of getting custody?

If you are seeing a therapist, you should feel comfort in knowing that you are obtaining the professional support you need. Your well-being is important to your ability to be the best parent you can be.

Discuss with your lawyer the implications of your being treated by a therapist. It may be that the condition for which you are being treated in no way affects your child or your ability to be a loving and supportive parent.

110

Because the mental and physical health of a parent is one factor is determining the best interest of the child, it may be possible for your spouse to obtain your mental health records. You may be asked to sign a release of record so that your mental health records may be subpoenaed by the other parent's lawyer. For this reason it is important to discuss with your attorney an action plan for responding to a request to obtain records in your therapist's file. Ask your attorney to contact your therapist to alert him or her regarding how to respond to a request for your mental health records.

8.12 I am taking prescription medication to treat my depression. Will this hurt my chances of having equal parenting time?

Not necessarily. Feelings of depression, anxiety, and trouble sleeping are common during a divorce. If you have any mental health concerns, seek help from a professional. Following through with the recommendations made by your health care provider will be looked favorably upon by the court, including the use of prescription medication.

If you are overusing prescription medication, or your medication prevents you from being able to care for the children, these are factors that may affect parenting time. Discuss the prescription medications you are taking with your attorney and whether you believe the medications have any effect on your ability to parent.

8.13 Will my children be present if we go to court?

No. Children are not permitted to be present in the courtroom to hear the testimony of other witnesses.

8.14 Should I hire a private detective to prove my spouse is having an affair?

Arizona is a no-fault state. Accordingly, the fact your spouse may be having an affair will not affect the judge's decision on whether to grant your spouse parenting time. However, if you believe the affair is affecting the children, talk with your lawyer about what evidence you might need to support your case.

8.15   Will the fact that I had an affair during the marriage hurt my chances of having significant parenting time?

Generally, the fact you had an affair will not affect the amount of parenting time you will receive. However, discuss with your attorney the following:

- Whether the children were exposed to the affair
- Whether the affair had any impact on the children
- How long ago the affair occurred

Your attorney can help you determine whether the affair will have any impact on your parenting time.

8.16   During the months it takes to get a divorce, is it okay to date or will it hurt my chances at obtaining equal parenting time?

If the amount of parenting time is disputed, talk with your attorney about your plans to begin dating. Your dating may be irrelevant if the children are unaware of it. However, exposing your children to a new relationship when they are still adjusting to the separation of their parents may not be in their best interest.

If your spouse is contesting the amount of parenting time you are requesting, it may be best to focus your energy on your children, the litigation, and taking care of yourself.

8.17   Can having a live-in partner hurt my chances of getting parenting time?

If you are contemplating having your partner live with you, discuss your decision with your attorney first. If you are already living with your partner, let your attorney know right away so that the potential impact on any custody ruling can be assessed.

Talk promptly and frankly with your lawyer. It will be important for you to look together at many aspects, including the following:

- Whether your living arrangement is likely to prompt a parenting time dispute that would not otherwise arise
- How long you have been separated from the parent
- How long you have been in a relationship with your new partner

- The history and nature of the children's relationship with your partner
- Your future plans with your partner (such as marriage)

Moving in with someone before a divorce is final often brings up issues that otherwise would not exist if you lived alone or continued to reside in the marital residence. Consider such a decision thoughtfully, taking into account the advice of your lawyer.

8.18   What impact will my sexual orientation have on my case for legal decision-making or parenting time?

There are no laws in Arizona that limit your rights as a parent based upon your sexual orientation. Your sexual orientation is not the same as your sexual activity.

Sexual activity by a parent, whether between heterosexual or same sex couples, is an insignificant factor in determining legal decision-making and parenting time. However, exposing your child to sexual activity or engaging in sexual activity that exposes your child to harm would be relevant factors in a parenting time dispute. The issue is the same as with other activities, such as alcohol or drug use or gambling. Action that exposes your child to potential physical or emotional harm will be considered by the court in determining legal decision-making and parenting time.

8.19   I believe my spouse is trying to alienate the children from me. What can I do?

One parent's attempt to align the children on his or her side against the other parent is unfortunately a common issue in divorce cases. Sometimes this alignment takes the form of a child siding with one parent over the other. Other times the alignment is more severe and results in parental alienation.

Parental alienation syndrome is the unwarranted rejection of one parent based upon the attitudes of the other parent. If parental alienation is present, the child will often refuse to see the other parent or will act out when at the other parent's residence. Oftentimes the child is rude, ungrateful, and cold toward the targeted parent. Oftentimes the child will completely cut off communication with the targeted parent.

If you believe that your child is exhibiting behaviors that appear to be based on an alignment with your spouse and alienation toward you, discuss this behavior with your attorney. The sooner this issue can be address and corrected, the more likely it will be to have far fewer consequences in the future.

8.20 Can I have witnesses speak on my behalf regarding parenting time for the minor children?

While witnesses can generally come forward and provide testimony, there is often not enough time to hear from a lot of different witnesses during a trial. In addition, the level of knowledge the witnesses have and how relevant that information is to legal decision-making and parenting time must be considered carefully.

Discuss with your lawyer which witnesses will be best for your particular case. Among those you might consider as potential witnesses in your case are:

- Family members
- Family friends
- Child-care providers
- Neighbors
- Teachers
- Health care providers
- Clergy members

In considering which witnesses would best support your case, your attorney may consider the following:

- What has been this witness's opportunity to observe you or the other parent, especially with your child?
- How frequently? How recently?
- How long has the witness known you or the other parent?
- What is the relationship of the witness to the child and the parents?
- How valuable is the knowledge that this witness has?
- Does this witness have knowledge different from that of other witnesses?
- Is the witness available and willing to testify?

- Is the witness clear in conveying information?
- Is the witness credible, that is, will the judge believe this witness?
- Does the witness have any biases or prejudices that could impact the testimony?

You and your attorney can work together to determine which witnesses will best support your case. Support your attorney by providing a list of potential witnesses together with your opinion regarding the answers to the questions above.

Give your attorney the phone numbers, addresses, and workplaces of each of your potential witnesses. This information can be critical to the role that the attorney has in interviewing the witnesses, contacting them regarding testifying, and issuing subpoenas to compel their court attendance if needed. When parents give conflicting testimony during a trial, the testimony of other witnesses can be key to determining the outcome of the case.

8.21   Will my attorney want to speak with my children?

In most cases your attorney will not ask to speak with your children. When one attorney speaks to the children, it puts the children in the middle of the divorce case, which should be avoided.

If you believe information from your child is important in your case, discuss this with your attorney. Your attorney may suggest having the child talk with a therapist, a court appointed advisor, or someone trained in appropriate interviewing techniques for children, especially for younger children.

8.22   Can my child have an attorney represent them in court?

The court may appoint an attorney to represent your child in the proceeding, or a best interest attorney may be assigned if the court finds at least one of the following:

- There is an allegation of abuse or neglect
- The parents are persistently in significant conflict with each other
- There is a history of substance abuse by either parent or family violence

- There are serious concerns about the mental health or behavior of either parent
- The child is an infant or toddler
- Or any other reason deemed appropriate by the judge

8.23 What is the difference between a *child's attorney* and a *best interest attorney*?

A *child's attorney* represents the child just as your attorney represents you. The child's attorney advocates for what their client (the child wants.)

A *best interest attorney* is appointed to conduct an investigation into what is in the best interest of the child. The best interest attorney participates in the proceeding to the same extent as an attorney for a party. The best interest attorney advocates for what he or she believes is in the best interest of the child, which may not necessarily be based on the child's wishes.

The court will determine the allocation of the fees and expenses between the parents if a child's attorney or best interest attorney is appointed.

8.24 I believe my spouse is not a fit parent. How can I help prove this to the court?

In some cases, it may be appropriate to have a court appointed advisor conduct an investigation, and in other cases it may be necessary to have what is still sometimes referred to as a *custody evaluation* performed by a mental health professional or other qualified individual.

A court appointed advisor may be asked by the court to investigate specific issues that arise during a case. For example, assume one allegation is that your spouse is living in a place where there is no pool fence, but your spouse denies this claim. A court appointed advisor may be appointed to conduct this very limited investigation.

Other times a court appointed advisor may be asked to look at the factors the court must consider in determining the best interest of a child. The court appointed advisor may speak with each parent, the child, school officials, and other potential witnesses in order to give the judge specific information about each factor.

The court appointed advisor will submit a report regarding the recommendations and the basis for the recommendation. In some cases, the court appointed advisor may be asked to testify as a witness at trial.

In other cases, it may be necessary to conduct a more formal family assessment. This assessment may be performed by a mental health professional who will perform a complete evaluation of the family. The expert may give psychological tests to determine if there are any issues either parent has that would affect parenting.

In addition, the mental health professional may meet with the parents, the child, and other potential witnesses. They may also want to see how the children interact with each parent and schedule time to see the children with each parent individually. The expert is also authorized to review and receive information, records, and reports concerning all parties involved.

When the mental health professional has completed his or her evaluation, they will prepare a report to submit to the court regarding their recommendations concerning legal decision-making and parenting time. The expert may also be asked to testify at trial.

8.25 How might photographs or a video of my child help my custody case?

Photographs or a video depicting your child's day-to-day life can help the judge learn more about your child's needs. It can demonstrate how your child interacts with you, siblings, and other important people in your family's life. The photographs or video can portray your child's room, home, and neighborhood, as well as show your child participating in activities.

Talk to your lawyer about whether photographs or a video would be helpful in your case. Although photographs are more commonly used and are typically sufficient evidence, ask your lawyer if he or she recommends making a video, and if so, what scenes to include, the length of the video, keeping the original tapes, and the editing process.

8.26 Can I provide audiotapes of my spouse if my spouse does not know that I taped them?

Arizona requires that only one party (the party taping) know that they are being recorded. Accordingly, it is possible to tape your spouse without their knowledge. However, prior to doing this, make sure to discuss this with your attorney and under what circumstances such an audiotape would be helpful to your case.

8.27 What does it mean to be an *unfit parent*?

Parental unfitness means that you have a personal deficiency or incapacity that will likely prevent you from performing essential parental obligations and is likely to result in a detriment to your child's well-being.

Determinations of your fitness to be a parent will largely depend upon the facts of your case. Reasons why a parent might be found to be unfit include a history of physical abuse, alcohol or drug abuse, or mental health problems that affect the ability to parent.

8.28 Does joint legal decision-making and parenting time always mean equal time at each parent's house?

No. Each parent may have continuous blocks of parenting time with the child for substantial lengths of time. However, this does not necessarily require that each parent have equal amounts of parenting time.

8.29 How might the days of the week be shared in an equal parenting time schedule?

There are multiple ways parties may share parenting time on an equal basis. A common way is a 2-2-3 plan. Under this plan, one parent has the child for two weekdays, then the other parent has the child for the following two weekdays, and then the child goes with the other parent for a three-day weekend. Here is an sample parenting chart to demonstrate the 2-2-3 schedule.

Sample 2-2-3 Parenting Time Schedule

	Monday	Tuesday	Wednesday	Thursday	Friday	Saturday	Sunday
Week 1	Parent 1 at 8 A.M.	Parent 1	Parent 2 Beginning at 5:00 P.M.	Parent 2	Parent 1 Beginning at 5:00 P.M.	Parent 1	Parent 1
Week 2	Parent 2 at 8 A.M.	Parent 2	Parent 1 Beginning at 5:00 P.M.	Parent 1	Parent 2 Beginning at 5:00 P.M.	Parent 2	Parent 2

As children get older, they may like more certainty on the days that they are at each parent's house. Under the 5-2-2-5 plan, a child still alternates weekends between the parents, but has every Monday and Tuesday with one parent and every Wednesday and Thursday with the other parent.

Some parents prefer to have a one week on, one week off parenting schedule. However, this schedule is generally not preferred because it takes the child away from the other parent for such an extended period of time.

The important thing is to devise a parenting plan that works for you, your spouse, and the children. In addition, some flexibility is required so the schedule can be modified to reflect special situations or so the children can attend certain events.

8.30   What is a *parenting plan*?

A *parenting plan* is a document detailing how you and your spouse will be parenting your child after the divorce. Among the issues addressed in a parenting plan are:

- Legal decision-making
- Parenting time, including specific times for:
  - Regular school year
  - Holidays
  - Birthdays
  - Mother's Day and Father's Day
  - Summer
  - School breaks
  - Three-day weekends
- Phone access to the child

119

- Communication regarding the child
- Access to records regarding the child
- Notice regarding parenting time
- Attendance at the child's activities
- Exchange of information such as addresses, phone numbers, and care providers

Detailed parenting plans are good for children and parents. They increase clarity for the parents, provide security for the child in knowing what to expect, reduce conflict, and lower the risk of needing to return to court for a modification of your divorce decree. A sample parenting plan concerning holidays is available the Appendix.

8.31 I don't think it's safe for my children to have any contact with my spouse. How can I prove this to the judge?

Keeping your children safe is so important that this discussion with your attorney requires immediate attention. Talk with your attorney about a plan for the protection of you and your children. Options might include an order of protection, supervised visitation, or certain restrictions on your spouse's parenting time, such as no overnight visitation. However, it is rare for the court to enter a no-contact order with respect to children absent extreme circumstances.

Give your attorney a complete history of the facts upon which you base your belief that your children are not safe with the other parent. Although the most recent facts are often the most relevant, it is important that your attorney have a clear picture of the background as well.

Your attorney also needs information about your spouse, such as whether your spouse is or has been:

- Using alcohol or drugs
- Treated for alcohol or drug use
- Arrested, charged, or convicted of crimes of violence
- In possession of firearms
- Subject to a protection order for harassment or violence

8.32 How can I get my spouse's parenting time to be supervised?

If you are concerned about the safety of your children when they are with your spouse, talk to your lawyer. It may be that an order of protection is warranted to terminate or limit contact with your children. Alternatively, it is possible to ask the judge to consider certain court orders intended to better protect your children.

Ask your attorney whether, under the facts of your case, the judge would consider any of the following court orders:

- Supervised visits
- Exchanges of the children in a public place
- Parenting class for the other parent
- Anger management or other rehabilitative program for the other parent
- A prohibition against drinking by the other parent when with the children

Judges have differing approaches to cases where children are at risk. Recognize that there are also often practical considerations, such as cost or the availability of people to supervise visits. Urge your attorney to advocate zealously for court orders to protect your children from harm by the other parent.

8.33 My spouse keeps saying he'll get the children because there were no witnesses to his abuse and I can't prove it. Is he right?

No. Most domestic violence is not witnessed by others, and judges know this.

If you have been a victim of abusive behavior by your spouse, or if you have witnessed your children as victims, your testimony is likely to be the most compelling evidence.

Be sure to tell your attorney about anyone who may have either seen your spouse's behavior or spoken to you or your children right after an abusive incident. They may be important witnesses in your case.

121

8.34   I am concerned about protecting my child from abuse by my spouse. Which types of past abuse by my spouse are important to tell my attorney?

Keeping your child safe is your top priority. So that your attorney can help you protect your child, give him or her a full history of the following behaviors of your spouse:

- Hitting, kicking, pushing, shoving, or slapping you or your child
- Sexual abuse
- Threats to harm you or the child
- Threats to abduct your child
- Destruction of property
- Torture of pets or harm to them
- Requiring your child to keep secrets

The process of writing down past events may help you to remember other incidents of abuse that you had forgotten. Be as complete as possible.

8.35   What documents or items should I give my attorney to help prove the history of domestic violence by my spouse?

The following may be useful exhibits if your case goes to court:

- Photographs of injuries
- Photographs of damaged property
- Abusive or threatening notes, letters, or e-mails
- Abusive or threatening voice messages
- Your journal entries about abuse
- Police reports
- Medical records
- Court records
- Criminal and traffic records
- Damaged property, such as torn clothing

Tell your attorney which of these you have or are able to obtain. Ask your lawyer whether other exhibits can be acquired through a subpoena or other means.

8.36 I want to talk to my spouse about our child, but all she wants to do is argue. How can I communicate without it always turning into a fight?

Because conflict is high between you and your spouse, consider the following:

- Ask your lawyer to help you obtain a court order for legal decision-making and parenting time that is specific and detailed. This lowers the amount of necessary communication between you and your spouse.
- Put as much information in writing as possible
- Consider using e-mail or mail, especially for less urgent communication
- Avoid criticisms of your spouse's parenting
- Avoid telling your spouse how to parent
- Be factual and business-like
- Acknowledge to your spouse the good parental qualities he or she displays, such as being concerned, attentive, or generous
- Keep your child out of any conflicts
- Consider using an online calendaring system to post important dates, medical appointments, and communications regarding your child's activities so that there can be no allegation that the other parent does not know what is happening

By focusing on your behavior, conflict with your spouse has the potential to decrease. Additionally, talk to your attorney about developing a communication protocol to follow when communicating with your spouse.

8.37 What if the child is not returned from parenting time at the agreed upon time? Should I call the police?

Calling the police should be done only as a last resort if you feel that your child is at risk for abuse or neglect, or if you have been advised by your attorney that such a call is warranted. The involvement of law enforcement officials in parental conflict can result in far greater trauma to a child than a late return at the end of a parenting time.

123

The appropriate response to a child not being returned according to a court order depends upon the circumstances. If the problem is a recurring one, talk to your attorney regarding your options. It may be that a change in the schedule would be in the best interest of your child.

Regardless of the behavior of the other parent, make every effort to keep your child out of any conflicts between the adults.

8.38   If I have sole legal decision-making, may I move out of state without the permission of the court?

Not necessarily. If by written agreement or court order, both parents are entitled to unsupervised parenting time and both parents reside in Arizona, notice must be given to the other parent. This notice must be given to the other parent in writing at least sixty days in advance before a parent may relocate out of state or more than a hundred miles.

In addition to being in writing, the notice must be by certified mail, return receipt requested. After the notice is given, it is up to the nonmoving parent to object.

If the nonmoving party objects, it must be done by filing a petition with the court within thirty days. If there is no objection within thirty days, then the court will allow an objection to prevent relocation only if there is good cause as to why the objection was not filed in a timely manner.

There are limited circumstances where you may be able to temporarily relocate with less than sixty day's notice. If you have sole decision-making and are required for health or safety or employment to relocate, you may temporarily relocate. Talk to your lawyer about the circumstances under which you may be able to temporarily relocate under these circumstances.

8.39   If my spouse and I have joint legal decision-making and substantially equal parenting time, are there any circumstances under which I can relocate out of state?

Yes. Although relocation cases are often the most difficult for judges, there is also a recognition that over time lives change, employment changes, and people remarry and need to move out of state.

You and your spouse may agree to a relocation and a long-distance parenting plan. If you both agree on the relocation, see your lawyer about making the necessary changes to the parenting plan.

If there is no agreement, you may either give the required sixty days' notice and see if your spouse objects or seek permission from the court to relocate. If you believe your spouse is likely to object, you may wish to seek permission from the court so you can have the issue addressed more quickly than waiting sixty days.

The court will determine whether you may relocate based upon the best interest of the children. Some of the factors the court considers are:

- The reasons for the relocation
- The prospective advantage of the move for improving the general quality of life for the parent or child
- The likelihood that the parent with whom the child resides will comply with parenting time orders after the relocation
- Whether the relocation will allow a realistic opportunity for parenting time with each parent
- The extent to which moving or not moving will affect the emotional, physical, or development needs of the child
- The potential effect of relocation on the child's stability

Talk with your lawyer about the possibility of obtaining a temporary order to relocate. In addition, it may be important to ask for an accelerated hearing so you will have a final court ruling determining whether you may move out of state with your child.

8.40   After the divorce, can my spouse legally take our children out of the state during parenting time? Out of the country?

It depends upon the terms of the court order as set forth in your decree. If you are concerned about your children being out of Arizona with the other parent, you may want some of these decree provisions regarding out-of-state travel with your child:

- Limits on the duration or distance for out-of-state travel with the child
- Notice requirements
- Information on phone numbers
- Information on physical addresses
- E-mail address contact information
- Possession of the child's passport with the court
- Posting of bond by the other parent prior to travel
- Requiring a court order for travel outside of the country

Although judges are not ordinarily concerned about short trips across state lines, you should let your attorney know if you are concerned that your child may be abducted by the other parent so that reasonable safeguards may be put in place.

8.41 If I am not given joint legal decision-making, what rights do I have regarding educational records, medical records, and medical treatment for my child?

Regardless of which parent has legal decision-making, both parents have the right to access their children's educational records, the medical records of their children, and to make emergency medical decisions.

8.42 If I do not have parenting time during the school week, how will I know what is going on at school?

Develop a relationship with your child's teachers and the school staff. Request to be put on the school's mailing list for all notices. Find out what is necessary for you to do to get copies of important school information and report cards.

Communicate with the other parent to both share and receive information about your child's progress in school. This will enable you to support your child and each other through any challenging periods of your child's education. It also enables you to share a mutual pride in your child's successes.

Regardless of which parent has parenting time during the school week, your child will benefit from your involvement in his or her education through your participation in parent-teacher conferences, attendance at school events, help with school homework, and positive communication with the other parent.

8.43 **If my spouse is awarded legal decision-making, can I still take my child to my place of religious worship during my parenting time?**

Yes. The decision of which religion the child should be is a fundamental decision that is made by the parent who has legal decision-making. If you have joint legal decision-making you will both make this decision. However, even if you do not have joint legal decision-making, as a parent you retain the authority to make day-to-day decisions for the child while he or she is in your care. This means that you can still take your child to religious activities during your parenting time.

8.44 **What if my child does not want to go for his or her parenting time? Can my former spouse force the child to go?**

If your child is resisting going with the other parent, it can first be helpful to determine the underlying reason. Consider these questions:

- What is your child's stated reason for not wanting to go?
- Does your child appear afraid, anxious, or sad?
- Do you have any concerns regarding your child's safety while with the other parent?
- Have you prepared your child for being with the other parent, speaking about the experience with enthusiasm and encouragement?
- Is it possible your child is perceiving your anxiety about the situation and is consequently having the same reaction?
- Have you provided support for your child's transition to the other home, such as completing fun activities in your home well in advance of the other parent's starting time for parenting?
- Have you spoken to the other parent about your child's behavior?
- Can you provide anything that will make your child's time with the other parent more comfortable, such as a favorite toy or blanket?

- Have you established clear routines that support your child to be ready to go with the other parent with ease, such as packing a backpack or saying goodbye to a family pet?

The reason for a child's reluctance to go with the other parent may be as simple as being sad about leaving you or as serious as being a victim of abuse in the other parent's home. It is important to look at this closely to determine the best response.

Judges treat compliance with court orders for parenting time seriously. If one parent believes that the other is intentionally interfering with parenting time or the parent-child relationship, it can result in further litigation. At the same time, you want to know that your child is safe. Talk with your attorney about the best approach in your situation.

8.45   If my spouse is not following the parenting plan, do I have to take my spouse back to court?

It is not unusual for problems to arise in the course of implementing a parenting plan. Sometimes it takes awhile for the routine to set in, and other times, parents may continue to have disputes.

These disputes can range from things such as not returning the child to the other on time to more serious issues such as which school the children will attend. In these cases, if both parties agree, it may be appropriate to have a parenting coordinator appointed in your case.

A *parenting coordinator* is an attorney or mental health professional who has received specified training. The order appointing the parenting coordinator will specify the scope. However, in general a parenting coordinator will attempt to help the parties resolve their issues with each other and, if unsuccessful, make recommendations to the court on the day-to-day issues experienced by parents.

A parenting coordinator does not have the authority to make recommendations affecting child support, a change in legal decision-making, or a substantial change in parenting time.

8.46   What steps can I take to prevent my spouse from getting the children in the event of my death?

Unless the other parent is not fit to have parenting time with the children, he or she will have first priority as the guardian of your child in the event of your death. All parents should have a will naming a guardian for their children. In the event you do not intend to name the other parent, talk with your attorney. Seek counsel about how to best document and preserve the evidence that will be needed to prove that the other parent is unfit to have legal decision-making or parenting time in the event of your death.

9

Child Support

Whether you will be paying or receiving child support is often the subject of much worry. Will you receive enough support to take care of your children? Will you have enough money to live on after you pay child support? How will you make ends meet?

Most parents want to provide for their children. Today, the child support laws make it possible for parents to have a better understanding of their obligation to support their children. The mechanisms for both payment and receipt of child support are more clearly defined, and help is available for collecting support if it's not paid.

The Arizona Child Support Guidelines and the Arizona Child Support Clearinghouse help to simplify the child support system. As you learn more about them, matters regarding child support that appeared complex in the beginning can eventually become routine for you and the other parent.

9.1 What determines whether I will receive child support?

Whether you will receive child support depends upon a number of factors. These include the income of each parent, how much time your child is living in your household, and which parent pays for health insurance, day care, or educational expenses.

If you have physical custody of your child, it is likely your spouse will be ordered to pay support for any children born or adopted during your marriage.

9.2 **Can I request child support even if I do not meet the ninety-day residency requirement for a divorce in Arizona?**

Yes. Even though you may not have met the requirements to obtain a divorce, you have a right to seek support for your children. You may file for a decree of legal separation so long as you are domiciled in the state at the time of the filing. By filing the decree of legal separation, you can seek a temporary order for child support.

In some cases, you may need to establish paternity or locate the noncustodial parent before you can establish a child support order. Talk to your attorney or visit the Arizona Department of Economic Security website at (www.azdes.gov/az_child_support) for contact information and to apply for child support services.

9.3 **Can I get temporary support while waiting for parenting time to be decided?**

A judge has authority to enter a temporary order for child support. This order ordinarily remains in place until a final decree establishing parenting time and child support is entered. In most cases a hearing for temporary parenting time and child support can be held shortly after the filing of the petition for dissolution or legal separation.

9.4 **What is *temporary child support* and how soon can I get it?**

Temporary child support is paid for the support of a child. It is determined sometime after the petition for dissolution is filed and continues until your final decree of divorce is entered by the court or until your case is dismissed.

If you are in need of temporary support, talk to your attorney at your first opportunity. Sometimes the parties are able to agree as to the temporary payment of support. Other times, it is necessary to seek a court order asking for support.

If you and your spouse are unable to agree upon the amount of temporary support to be paid each month, talk to your attorney. If an agreement is not reached, it is likely that your attorney will file a motion for temporary support asking the judge to decide how much the support should be and when it will start.

Because there are a number of steps for obtaining a temporary child support order, do not delay in discussing your need for support with your lawyer.

The following are the common steps in the process:

- You discuss your need for a temporary child support with your lawyer.
- Your lawyer requests a hearing date from the judge and prepares the necessary documents.
- A temporary hearing is held.
- The temporary order is signed by the judge.
- Your spouse's employer is notified to begin withholding your support from your spouse's paychecks.
- Your spouse's employer sends the support to the Arizona Support Clearinghouse.
- The clearinghouse sends the money to you.

If your spouse is not paying you support voluntarily, time is of the essence in obtaining a temporary order for support. This should be one of the first issues you discuss with your lawyer.

Even if a temporary order is not requested, the court at the time of the final decree will enter an order for retroactive child support. The child support will be retroactive to the date of filing the petition for dissolution or legal separation.

In some cases, if you have lived separate and apart from your spouse before a petition for dissolution or legal separation is filed, the court may order child support retroactive to the date of separation, but not more than three years prior.

9.5 How soon does my spouse have to start paying support for the children?

Your spouse may begin paying you support voluntarily at any time. A temporary order for support will give you the right to collect the support if your spouse stops paying. Talk to your lawyer about court hearings for temporary support in your county. You may have to wait a number of weeks before your temporary orders hearing can be held. It is possible that the judge will not order child support to start until the first month following the hearing.

9.6 How is the amount of child support I'll receive or pay figured?

The Arizona Child Support Guidelines (A.R.S. §25-320) were adopted by the Arizona Supreme Court to set forth the standards by which your child support is calculated. According to the guidelines, both parents have a duty to contribute to the support of their children in proportion to their respective gross incomes. As a result, both your income and the income of your spouse will factor into the child support calculation.

Other factors the court may consider include:

- The financial resources and needs of the child
- The financial resources and needs of the custodial parent
- The standard of living the child would have enjoyed if the child lived in an intact home with both parents
- The physical and emotional condition of the child and the child's educational needs
- The financial resources and needs of the noncustodial parent
- The medical support plan for the child
- Excessive or abnormal expenditures, destruction, concealment or fraudulent disposition of community, joint tenancy, and other property held in common
- The duration of parenting time and related expenses

Child support that is higher or lower than what the guidelines provide for may be awarded in certain cases, for example:

- When either parent or child has extraordinary medical costs
- When a child has special health or education needs
- Whenever the application of the guidelines in an individual case would be unjust or inappropriate

When a judge orders an amount of support that is different from the guideline amount, it is referred to as a *deviation*.

Due to the complexity of calculations under the guidelines, computer software is used to calculate child support. You can review the guidelines in greater detail at (www.azcourts. gov/familylaw/arizonachildsupportguidelines.aspx).

You may also fill out a child support work sheet to determine your basic child support amount by visiting (www. azcourts.gov/familylaw/2011childsupportcalculator.aspx).

9.7 Will the amount of parenting time I have impact the amount of child support I receive?

It can. Having an equal parenting time schedule can dramatically lower child support amounts. For this reason, it is essential that you discuss child support with your attorney prior to reaching any agreements with your spouse regarding parenting time.

If you intend to mediate parenting time, be sure to talk with your attorney in advance regarding how it can affect your child support.

9.8 Is overtime pay considered in the calculation of child support?

Yes, if your overtime is a routine part of your employment that you can actually expect to earn regularly. The judge can consider your work history, the degree of control you have over your overtime, and the nature of the field in which you work.

9.9 Will rental income be factored into my child support or just my salary?

Yes. Income from other sources may be considered in determining the amount of child support. However, if the payment is a one-time payment and is not likely to reoccur, such as a one-time insurance settlement, this may not be calculated into child support. Be sure to advise your attorney of all sources of income in order to determine which amounts are considered in determining child support.

9.10 My spouse has a college degree but refuses to get a job. Will the court consider this in determining the amount of child support?

The *earning capacity* of your spouse may be considered instead of current income. The court can look at your spouse's work history, education, skills, health, and job opportunities. The court will also look at whether your spouse has voluntarily quit his or her job or reduced his or her income shortly before a determination on child support. This may be considered in determining whether actual income or earning capacity should be used for calculation of support.

If you believe your spouse is earning substantially less than the income he or she is capable of earning, provide your attorney with details. Ask about making a case for child support based on earning capacity instead of actual income.

9.11 Will I get the child support directly from my spouse or from the state?

If the payor parent is employed, an order of assignment will be issued by the court that will direct the payer's employer to withhold income from the employee's paycheck. After the order of assignment is in effect, child support will be withheld and sent to the Arizona Child Support Clearinghouse for payment to the parent receiving support. Employers routinely withhold child support from employee wages just as they withhold taxes or retirement.

If a parent is self-employed or if income is not being withheld by his or her employer, the parent makes child support payments to the Arizona Support Payment Clearinghouse. The payment center then sends the child support to the parent receiving support. Payments can be mailed to: Arizona Support Payment Clearinghouse, P.O. Box 52107, Phoenix, Arizona 85072-2107.

Information on how to pay electronically or over the telephone can be found by calling the Arizona Payment Gateway at (866) 562-0140, the Arizona Department of Child Support Services at (602) 252-4045, or toll-free in Arizona at (800) 882-4150.

9.12   How will I receive my child support payment?

The Arizona Support Payment Clearinghouse has several methods of disbursing your child support money. The Clearinghouse can send your child support check in the mail. However, it may take five to ten business days for processing through the mail. This timeframe may be even longer if it is an out-of-state check or a certified check.

You can also receive your payment by direct deposit so that your child support payment is automatically deposited into your bank account. Additionally, your child support can be deposited directly onto an electronic payment card, which operates as a debit card. With the electronic payment card, your child support payments will be transferred electronically into your card account, from which you can access your money at any Automated Teller Machine (ATM) and is accepted anywhere debit cards are accepted. Receiving your child support payment by direct deposit or by an electronic payment card is the fastest way to obtain your payments.

More information can be found at (www.azcourts.gov/familylaw/ChildSupportFrequentlyAskedQuestions) and at the Arizona Department of Economic Security website at (www.azdes.gov/az_child_support).

9.13   Is there any reason not to pay or receive payments directly to or from my spouse after the court has entered a child support order?

Yes. After a child support order is entered by the court, the Arizona Support Payment Clearinghouse keeps a record of all support paid. If the payment is not made through the clearinghouse, the state's records will show that the paying spouse is behind in child support.

Direct payments of child support may be considered a gift to the other spouse rather than child support. The payer may have intended the money to pay a child support payment, but the parent receiving the support may have thought it was extra money to help with the child's expenses.

The payment of support through the clearinghouse protects both parents. If a direct payment is made, be sure a notarized receipt is signed and filed with the clerk of the superior court in which your child support order was entered.

This is important so that the state's records remain accurate. If no receipt is filed for a direct payment, it may later be considered a gift.

9.14   I understand I have to have an *ATLAS number*. What is that?

ATLAS stands for *Arizona Tracking and Location Automatic System*. This is a twelve-digit number that is assigned to each child support order by the Arizona Division of Child Support Enforcement.

After assigned, the number is used to track the payment of child support. All checks paid to the clearinghouse should include the payee's name on the check and the ATLAS number for tracing of payments.

9.15   How soon can I expect my child support payments to start arriving?

A number of factors may affect the date on which you will begin receiving your child support. Here are the usual steps in the process:

- A child support amount and start date for the support are decided either by agreement between you and your spouse or by the judge.

- An *income withholding order* is completed and an *order of assignment* is issued by the court.

- An ATLAS number is assigned.

- Your spouse's employer withholds the support from the paycheck.

- The child support is transferred by the employer to the Arizona Support Payment Clearinghouse.

- The clearinghouse sends the money to you, usually by direct deposit or an electronic debit card.

As you can see, there are a number of steps in this process. Plan your budget knowing that the initial payment of child support might be delayed.

9.16 Will some amount of child support be withheld from every paycheck?

It depends upon the employer's policy and how you are paid. If support is due on the first of the month, the employer has the full month to withhold the amount ordered to be paid. If an employer issues paychecks twice a month, it is possible that half of the support will be withheld from each check and paid to the clearinghouse as withheld.

If an employer issues checks every other week, which is twenty-six pay periods per year, there will be some months in which a third paycheck is issued. Consequently, it is possible that no child support will be withheld from the wages paid in that third check of the month or that some checks will be for less than 50 percent of the monthly amount due.

For example: Suppose child support is $650 per month. Payer is paid every other Friday, or twenty-six times per year. The employer may withhold $300 per paycheck for child support. Although most months the support received will be $600, for a few months it will be $900. By the end of the year, however, the payer will have paid the same amount as if $650 had been paid each month.

Over time, child support payments typically fall into a routine schedule, which makes it easier for both the payer and the recipient of support to plan their budgets.

9.17 If my spouse has income other than from an employer, is it still possible to get a court order to withhold my child support from his income?

Yes. Child support can be automatically withheld from most sources of income. These may include unemployment, worker's compensation, retirement plans, and investment income.

9.18 The person I am divorcing is not the biological parent of my child. Can I still collect child support from my spouse?

In general, a stepparent is not liable for child support. Only biological or adoptive parents have a duty of support.

Discuss the facts of your case in detail with your lawyer. When you are clear about what will be in the best interest of your child, your attorney can support you in developing a strategy for your case that takes into consideration not only child support but also the future relationship of your spouse with your child.

9.19 Can I collect child support from both the biological parent and the adoptive parent of my child?

When your child was adopted, the biological parent's duty to support your child ended. However, it may be possible for you to collect past due child support from the period of time before the adoption.

9.20 What happens with child support when our children go to the other parent's home for summer vacation? Is child support still due?

Yes. Child support is calculated based upon the number of parenting days. Accordingly, the fact that the other parent may have extended parenting time during the summer is already calculated in the number of parenting days.

9.21 After the divorce, if I choose to remarry, can I still collect child support?

Yes. Although spousal maintenance will end if you remarry, child support does not terminate for this reason.

9.22 Will my new spouse's income be considered for child support?

Generally, only your income is considered. However, speak with your lawyer if you remarry because income for child support is considered income from any source and includes noncash benefits and recurring gifts. The funds your new spouse may be contributing toward your household expenses or living expenses may become relevant.

9.23 Can I still collect child support if I move to another state?

Yes. A move out of state will not end your right to receive child support. However, the amount of child support could be changed if other circumstances change, such as income or costs for exercising parenting time.

9.24 How long can I expect to receive child support?

Under Arizona law, child support is ordinarily ordered to be paid until the child reaches the age of eighteen and has graduated from high school. If a child turn eighteen while still in high school, child support continues until the child graduates from high school but only until the child reaches nineteen.

Child support will also cease if the child dies or is legally emancipated (that is declared self-supporting by the court and neither parent has any further financial liability to the child).

9.25 Can child support last longer if my child has special needs?

It depends. The court must make special findings that the child is severely mentally or physically disabled as demonstrated by the fact that the child is not able to live independently. The court must find that this disability began before the child reached the age of majority.

Talk with your lawyer if you believe your child has special needs. Your lawyer will advise you as to the evidence that must be presented to the court so that child support may continue past the age of majority.

9.26 Does interest accrue on past-due child support?

Yes, interest accrues on past due child support. Currently, interest accrues at the rate of 10 percent on each unpaid payment. Interest will be tracked by the clearinghouse.

9.27 What can I do if my former spouse refuses to pay child support?

There are two different methods for enforcement of child support obligations. Both methods may be pursued simultaneously.

If your former spouse is not paying child support, you may take action to enforce the court order with the help of your lawyer. Your lawyer may advise filing a *petition for contempt* for non-payment of support. If the petition is granted by the court, the court will order that a certain amount be paid immediately in order to purge the contempt order. Regular payments may also be required to be made until the arrearages are paid in full.

In addition, the Child Support Services section of the Attorney General's office also may assist you in enforcing your child support order. Visit the website at (www.azdes.gov/dcse). An application for services may be found at (www.azdes.gov/InternetFiles/InternetProgrammaticForms/pdf/cs167en22.pdf).

To review, if you are not receiving child support, you have two options:

- Call your attorney.
- Visit the Department of Economic Security websites listed previously.

9.28 At what point will the state help me collect back child support, and what methods do they use?

It depends. Individuals who receive assistance under the *Temporary Assistance to Needy Families* or federally assisted *Foster Care or Medical Assistance Only* programs automatically receive child support services. If you do not receive any state or federal assistance, you can receive services by completing an application.

You must initiate contact with the state if you want help collecting your child support. You should do so as soon as child support becomes delinquent by more than a couple of months. Otherwise the amount of back support may become so great that it could take years for you to obtain the full amount owed.

9.29 I live outside of Arizona. Will the money I spend on airline tickets to see my children impact my child support?

It might. If you expect to spend large sums of money for transportation in order to have parenting time with your children, talk to your attorney about how this might be taken into consideration when determining the amount of child support.

9.30 After the divorce, can my former spouse substitute buying sprees with the child for child support payments?

No. Purchases of gifts and clothing for a child do not relieve your former spouse from an obligation to pay you child support.

9.31 Are child-care expenses supposed to be taken out of my child support?

It depends. If you have continuing and regular child-care costs (such as day care expenses), sometimes you and your spouse will agree that you will each share a proportional amount of the costs.

The child care costs also may be added to the child support work sheet so that it is considered in determining the amount of child support each parent owes. In addition, if you have the majority of parenting time, and you pay for child care, you may be eligible for a credit from federal tax liability for child-care costs for dependent children.

9.32 How does providing health insurance for my child affect my child support amount?

If you pay the health insurance premium for your child, the amount you pay will be taken into account when calculating child support. You will receive a credit for the amount you pay per month for your child's health insurance premium.

9.33 Am I required to pay for my child's unreimbursed medical expenses from the child support I receive?

Yes, unless your decree provides otherwise. Otherwise, the percentage each party is required to pay of the unreimbursed medical expenses will be provided on the child support work sheet prepared by the court.

9.34 Am I required to pay for the general, everyday expenses for my child with the child support I receive?

Yes, if you are receiving child support, under the guidelines, you are responsible for expenses for your child such as housing, clothing, and food when you're your child is residing with you.

The other parent will pay for the everyday expenses of housing, clothing, and food when the child is in their care. You will need to coordinate with the other parent for purchases of major expenses.

9.35 Can my spouse be required by the decree to pay for our child's private elementary and high school education?

It depends. School choice is often a very heated discussion between parents. If the children are currently attending private school, and the parties can continue to afford to send the children to private school, the court may order one or both parents to pay.

If you and your spouse settle your case in advance of trial, it is a good idea to include in your consent decree and property settlement agreement a provision for payment of such tuition to avoid future disputes.

If you want your spouse to share this expense for your child, talk it over with your lawyer. Be sure to provide your attorney with information regarding tuition, fees, and other expenses related to private education.

9.36 Can my spouse be required by the decree to contribute financially to our child's college education?

The legal duty of a parent to support a child does not include payment for college education. However, if your spouse agrees to pay this expense, it can be included in the final decree and it will be an enforceable court order. Such a provision is ordinarily included in a divorce decree only as a result of a negotiated settlement.

If your decree includes a provision for payment of college education expenses, be sure it is specific. Terms to consider include:

- What expenses are included? For example, tuition, room and board, books, fees, or travel abroad
- Is there a limit? For example, up to the level of the cost of attendance at one of the in-state universities or a certain dollar amount
- When is the payment due?
- For what period of time does it continue?
- Are there any limits on the type of education that will be paid for?

- Is there a requirement that the child keep a certain grade point average to continue to receive parental assistance?

The greater the clarity in such a provision, the lower the risk is for misunderstanding or conflict years later.

10

Spousal Maintenance

Arizona uses the term *spousal maintenance* for what you commonly think of as *alimony.* The mere mention of the words spousal maintenance or alimony might stir your emotions and start your stomach churning. If your spouse has filed for divorce and is seeking spousal maintenance, you might see it as a double injustice—your marriage is ending and you feel like you have to pay for it, too. If you are seeking spousal maintenance, you might feel hurt and confused that your spouse is resistant to helping support you, even though you may have interrupted your career to stay home and care for your children.

Learning more about Arizona's laws on spousal maintenance, also sometimes referred to as *spousal support,* can help you move from your emotional reaction to the reality of possible outcomes in your case. Uncertainty about the precise amount of support that may be awarded or the number of years it might be paid is not unusual. Work closely with your lawyer. Be open to possibilities. Try looking at it from your spouse's perspective.

With the help of your lawyer, you will know the best course of action to take toward a spousal maintenance decision you can live with after your divorce is over.

10.1 Which gets calculated first, child support or spousal maintenance?

Spousal maintenance. Child support is determined from the income of both parties, which may include the amount of income deducted if you pay spousal support, and the amount you receive if you are receiving support.

10.2 What's the difference between *spousal maintenance, alimony* and *spousal support*?

In Arizona, spousal maintenance, alimony and spousal support have the same meaning.

10.3 How will I know if I am eligible to receive spousal maintenance?

Talk with your attorney about whether you are a candidate for spousal maintenance.

Under Arizona law to be eligible for spousal maintenance you must meet one of the following five factors:

- You will lack sufficient property after the divorce to support your reasonable needs.

- You are unable to be support yourself through appropriate employment after the divorce, or if you have young children whose age or condition is such that you need to care for them and should not be required to seek outside employment or you lack earning ability in the workforce adequate to be self-sufficient

- You made a significant financial or other contribution to the education, training, vocational skills, career, or earning ability of your spouse

- You had a long-term marriage and you are of an age that may preclude the possibility of gaining employment adequate to be self-sufficient

- You significantly reduced your income or career opportunities for the benefit of your spouse

Meeting one of these factors qualifies you for spousal maintenance, but the judge must still consider other factors to determine the amount and duration of support.

10.4   If I qualify for spousal maintenance how much will I receive?

Judges have various opinions as to the amount and duration of spousal maintenance. Assuming you qualify for spousal maintenance by meeting one of the five conditions stated previously, the judge will then look at thirteen other factors in determining the amount and duration of spousal maintenance. These factors are as follows:

- The standard of living established during the marriage
- The duration of the marriage
- Your age, employment history, earning ability, and physical and emotional condition
- The ability of your spouse to pay maintenance while meeting his or her own needs
- The comparative financial resources of each spouse, including the comparative earning abilities of each spouse
- Your contribution to the earning ability of your spouse
- The extent to which you have reduced your income or career opportunities for the benefit of your spouse
- The ability of both parents to contribute to the future educational costs of your children
- The financial resources of the party seeking maintenance, including the marital property apportioned to you and your ability to meet your own needs independently
- The time necessary to acquire sufficient education or training to enable you to find appropriate employment and whether such education or training is readily available
- Whether there have been excessive or abnormal expenditures, destruction, concealment or fraudulent disposition of community, joint tenancy, and other property held in common
- The costs for you to obtain health insurance and the reduction in health insurance paid by your spouse on your behalf

- All actual damages and judgments from conduct that results in criminal conviction of either spouse in which the other spouse or child was the victim

As you can tell from the number of factors that a court must consider, every case for spousal maintenance will be unique. Providing your lawyer with clear and detailed information about the facts of your marriage and current situation will allow him or her to make a spousal maintenance assessment in your case.

10.5 What information should I provide to my attorney if I want spousal maintenance?

If your attorney advises you that you may qualify for spousal maintenance, be sure to provide complete facts about your situation, including:

- A history of the interruptions in your education or career for the benefit of your spouse, including transfers or moves due to your spouse's employment
- A history of the interruptions in your education or career for raising children, including periods during which you worked part-time
- Your complete educational background, including the dates of your schooling or training and degrees earned
- Your work history, including the names of your employers, the dates of your employment, your duties, your pay, and the reasons you left
- Any pensions or other benefits lost due to the interruption of your career for the benefit of the marriage
- Your health history, including any current diagnoses, treatments, limitations, and medications
- Your monthly living expenses, including anticipated future expenses such as health insurance and taxes
- A complete list of the debts for you and your spouse
- Income for you and your spouse, including all sources

Also include any other facts that might support your need for spousal maintenance, such as other contributions you made to the marriage, upcoming medical treatment, or a lack of jobs in the field in which you were formerly employed.

148

No two spousal support cases are alike. The better the information your lawyer has about your situation, the easier it will be for him or her to assess your case.

10.6 My attorney told me I need to fill out an *affidavit of financial information*. What is this?

In every case where a spouse is seeking spousal maintenance, both parties must fill out an *affidavit of financial information (AFI)*. An affidavit of financial information is a court form that details your income and expenses on a daily basis.

An AFI is usually done at least twice, if not more during the proceedings. Usually, it is done at the beginning of the case to help determine whether support should be paid, or can be paid, on a temporary basis. The court also requires you to file an updated AFI prior to trial. If there are no minor children, the sections on children expenses may be skipped. A copy of an affidavit of financial information is included in the Appendix.

10.7 What if I do not have all the information I need to fill out the affidavit of financial information?

Many times, especially at the beginning of the case, it is hard to know all the expenses you are likely to incur. Go over the affidavit with your attorney, who will help to answer the questions for you. Sometimes it may be necessary to estimate expenses until you have a more complete understanding of your financial situation.

10.8 What is a *vocational evaluation*?

If a spouse has been out of the workforce for a number of years, either one or both sides may want to have a *vocational evaluation*. A vocational evaluation is performed by a qualified individual who can analyze your earning ability in the workforce. The purpose is to help determine how much the spouse seeking maintenance can earn if they were to go back into the workforce and attempt to find employment.

The evaluation takes into consideration the spouse's current level of education and skills. A determination is then made as to what the spouse might be able to do in the workplace, whether additional training is needed and how long it would take, and how much income the spouse is expected to earn.

10.9 My spouse told me that because I had an affair during the marriage, I have no chance to get spousal maintenance. Is it true that I have no case?

No. Arizona is a no-fault state. Infidelity is not considered by the court in granting or denying spousal maintenance. However, excessive or abnormal expenditures are a factor the court considers in awarding the amount and duration of spousal maintenance.

If your affair had a financial impact on the marital estate so that it could be considered an excess or abnormal expenditure, it may be taken into consideration when determining the amount of spousal maintenance. Be honest with your attorney if you have had an affair so your attorney can advise you how this might affect your case.

10.10 How is the amount of spousal maintenance calculated?

Unlike child support, there are not specific guidelines for determining the amount and duration of spousal maintenance. A judge will look at the expenses and incomes of you and your spouse, after giving consideration to the factors set forth in question 10.4.

Judges are given a lot of discretion to make their own decision on spousal maintenance without the benefit of specific guidelines. Consequently, the outcome of a spousal maintenance ruling by a judge can be one of the most unpredictable aspects of your divorce.

10.11 My spouse makes a lot more money than he reports on our tax return, but he hides it. How can I prove my spouse's real income to show he can afford to pay spousal maintenance?

Alert your attorney to your concerns. Your lawyer can then take a number of actions to determine your spouse's income with greater accuracy. They are likely to include:

- Subpoena of bank information and credit card statements to determining how money is spent

- An examination of check registers and bank deposits
- Depositions of third parties who have knowledge of income or spending by your spouse
- Subpoena of records of places where your spouse has made large purchases or received income
- Comparison of income claimed with expenses paid
- Inquiries of purchases made in cash

By partnering with your lawyer, you may be able to build a case to establish your spouse's actual income as greater than is shown on tax returns. If you filed joint tax returns, discuss with your lawyer any other implications of erroneous information on those returns.

10.12 I want to be sure the records on the spousal maintenance I pay are accurate, especially for tax purposes. What's the best way to ensure this?

If you are paying child support in addition to spousal support, both support payments should be made to the Arizona Support Payment Clearinghouse.

If you pay spousal maintenance but no child support, you may still make your payments directly to the Arizona Support Payment Clearinghouse. This is the best way to avoid any misunderstanding or claims that payments were not paid or not made on time. Spousal maintenance can be automatically withheld from your pay, just like your child support.

By avoiding direct payments to your former spouse, you and he or she will have accurate records. If you do pay directly, ask your spouse to sign an acknowledgment of direct payment.

10.13 What effect does spousal maintenance have on my taxes?

Your spousal maintenance payments are no longer tax deductible. Likewise, if you receive spousal maintenance, you do not pay income tax on the amount received. For more information, please *see* questions 14.4 and 14.5 in chapter 14.

10.14 What types of payments are considered spousal maintenance?

Payments to a third party on behalf of your spouse under the terms of your divorce decree may be treated as spousal maintenance. These may include payments for your spouse's medical expenses, housing costs, taxes, and tuition. These payments are treated as if they were received by your spouse then paid to the third party. Additionally, if you pay the premiums on a life insurance policy that is owned by your spouse, those payments may be considered spousal maintenance. Finally, if you are ordered to pay for expenses for a house owned by you and your spouse, some of your payments may be considered spousal maintenance.

10.15 How is the purpose of spousal maintenance different from the payment of my property settlement?

Spousal maintenance and the division of property serve two distinct purposes. The purpose of spousal maintenance is to provide support. In contrast, the purpose of a property division is to distribute the marital assets equitably between you and your spouse. You should not have to deplete the property divided in the divorce in order to support your needs.

10.16 My spouse makes a lot more money than I do. Will I be awarded spousal maintenance to make up the difference in our income?

Although the purpose of spousal maintenance is to provide support, such awards are not used to equalize the incomes of the parties. Instead, support may be awarded to assist the economically disadvantaged spouse for the transitional period during and after the divorce, until he or she becomes economically self-sufficient. However, a disparity in income is one factor the judge contemplates when considering an award of spousal maintenance.

10.17 How long can I expect to receive support?

Like your right to receive support, how long you will receive spousal support will depend upon the facts of your case and the judge's philosophy. In general, the longer your marriage, the stronger your case is for a long-term spousal maintenance award.

You may receive only short-term rehabilitative spousal maintenance to help bridge where you are at in your career now and where you expect to be within a short period of time, or you may receive spousal maintenance for several years. Talk to your attorney about the facts of your case to get a clearer picture of the possible outcomes in your situation. Unless you and your spouse agree otherwise, your spousal maintenance will terminate upon your remarriage or the death of either of you.

10.18 Does remarriage affect my spousal maintenance?

Yes. Under Arizona law, unless your divorce decree provides otherwise, spousal maintenance ends upon the remarriage of the recipient.

10.19 Does the death of my former spouse affect my spousal maintenance?

Yes. Under Arizona law, unless your decree provides otherwise, spousal maintenance ends upon the death of either party. That's why if you settle your case, you should negotiate a provision that your spouse must at all times keep enough life insurance in place for your benefit in at least the amount of any remaining spousal maintenance owed to you.

10.20 Do I have to keep paying spousal maintenance if my former spouse is now living with a new significant other?

Yes. Do not stop making your spousal maintenance payments. Instead, contact your attorney to see if it is possible to seek a modification of the spousal maintenance award. Support may be reduced or terminated with a new court order if your former spouse is living with a new significant other and his or her living expenses have significantly decreased.

10.21 Can I continue to collect spousal maintenance if I move to a different state?

Yes. The duty of your former spouse to follow a court order to pay spousal maintenance does not end simply because you move to another state, unless this is a specific provision in your decree.

10.22 What can I do if my spouse stops paying spousal maintenance?

If your spouse stops paying spousal maintenance, see your attorney about your options for enforcing your court order. The judge may order the support be taken from a source of your spouse's income or from a financial account belonging to your spouse.

If your spouse is intentionally refusing to pay spousal support, talk to your attorney about whether pursuing a *contempt of court action* would be effective. In a contempt action, your spouse may be ordered to appear in court and provide evidence explaining why support has not been paid. Possible consequences for contempt of court include a jail sentence or a fine.

10.23 Can I return to court to modify spousal maintenance?

It depends. If your divorce decree provides that your spousal maintenance order is "nonmodifiable," then it may not be modified. Also, your decree may not be modified to award spousal maintenance if spousal maintenance was not awarded in the original decree dissolving the marriage.

If there has been a change in circumstances that is substantial and continuing for either you or your spouse, you may seek to have spousal maintenance modified. Examples include a serious illness or the loss or obtaining of a job.

A request to modify spousal maintenance for the purposes of seeking spousal maintenance may not be filed if the time for payment of spousal maintenance allowed under your original decree has already passed.

If you think you have a basis to modify your support, contact your attorney at once to be sure a timely modification request is filed with the court.

10.24 Can spousal maintenance become "fixed" or "non-modifiable"?

Yes. Although the judge cannot order spousal maintenance to be nonmodifiable, you and your spouse can agree that spousal maintenance will not be modifiable in the amount and duration agreed to in your property settlement agreement. This is a complex issue that you must discuss with your attorney.

11

Division of Property

You and your spouse built a life together. You equally managed and purchased assets and items that you accumulated over many years. They were part of your home and your life. You never imagined that there would come a time when you would have to decide which items you wanted to keep and which you would have to let go.

Nor did you probably ever image that you could face losing the house you and your spouse so happily moved into—the house where you celebrated family traditions and spent countless hours making it "home." Your spouse wants it and your lawyer says it might have to be sold.

During a divorce, you will decide whether you or your spouse will take ownership of everything from bathroom towels to the stock portfolio. Suddenly, you find yourself having a strong attachment to that lamp in the family room or the painting in the hallway. Why does the collection of coins suddenly take on new meaning?

Your lawyer will help you do your best to reach agreement regarding dividing household goods. Other assets may need to be valued by an expert, such as the family business or real estate. From tax consequences to replacement value, there are many factors to consider in deciding whether to fight to keep an asset, to give it to your spouse, or to have it sold.

Like all aspects of your divorce, take one step at a time. By starting with the items most easily divided, you and your spouse can avoid paying lawyers to litigate the value of that 1980s album collection.

11.1   What system does Arizona use for dividing property?

Arizona is a community property state. *Community property* means that each spouse holds a one-half interest in property acquired during the marriage, with certain exceptions. Property acquired by gift, inheritance, or bequest are considered separate property of the spouse acquiring the property.

In a divorce, community property will be divided equitably, though not necessarily in kind, without regard to marital misconduct. In general, this means that all the community property will be divided in half, and each spouse will receive equal value for the property that they are relinquishing. For example, if one spouse receives the family vehicle with a value of $12,000, the other spouse will receive property worth $12,000.

11.2   How does community property division differ from other states?

Some states use equitable distribution for division of property. Equitable distribution provides for an equitable or fair, but not necessarily equal, division of the property and debts acquired during your marriage.

Regardless of how title is held, the court in equitable distribution states can use its discretion to make a division of the marital assets and marital debts. Although this may mean an equal division, it can also mean that an unequal division may still be considered "equitable."

11.3   What does *separate property* mean?

Separate property is any property acquired before the marriage, as well as property acquired during the marriage by gift, inheritance, or bequest. In addition, property acquired after service of the petition for dissolution of marriage or petition for legal separation is considered separate property if a decree of dissolution or legal separation is actually entered.

11.4   How is it determined who gets the house?

The first issue to be decided regarding the family home is the determination of who will retain possession of it while the divorce is pending. Later, it must be decided whether the house will be sold or whether it will be awarded to you or your spouse.

Several factors to consider when determining the disposition of the home are:

- How title to the home is held
- Who can afford the mortgage and expenses associated with the home
- Whether it is possible to refinance the home in order to take the other party off the mortgage
- Whether there are other assets in the marital estate to offset the value of the home

Talk with your lawyer about your options and to consider the listed factors. If you and your spouse are unable to reach agreement regarding the house, the judge will decide who keeps the home or whether the home will be sold and how the proceeds will be divided.

11.5   Should I sell the house during the divorce proceedings?

Selling your home is a big decision. To help you decide what is right for you, ask yourself these questions:

- What will be the impact (positive or negative) on my children if the home is sold?
- Can I afford to stay in the house after the divorce?
- After the divorce, will I be willing to give the house and yard the time, money, and physical energy required for its maintenance?
- Is it necessary for me to sell the house to pay a share of the equity to my spouse, or are there other options?
- Would my life be easier if I were in a smaller or simpler home?
- Would I prefer to move closer to the support of friends and family?
- What is the state of the housing market in my community?
- What are the benefits of remaining in this house?
- Can I retain the existing mortgage or will I have to refinance?

- Will I have a higher or lower interest rate if I sell the house and buy a new one?
- Can I see myself living in a different home?
- Will I have the means to acquire another home?
- If I don't retain the home and my spouse asks for it, what effect will this have on my custody case?
- Will my spouse agree to the sale of the house?
- What will be the real estate commission?
- What will be the costs of preparing the house for sale?

Selling a home is more than just a legal or financial decision. Consider what is important to you in creating your life after divorce when deciding whether to sell your home.

11.6 Should I try to keep the home to avoid any negative impact on the children?

Many times the first instinct is to want to keep the home especially if there are minor children. Sometimes you may be reluctant to sell the home until the children have completed high school because of the fear it will disrupt their lifestyle.

Careful thought should be given prior to making a decision on the house. Children are very flexible and sometimes the fact that the family home is kept by one parent can be more detrimental. The house now becomes the home that either mother or father left and their absence is more pronounced.

When both parties move to new homes, it gives the minor children an opportunity to see that they have two homes now, versus the home they have always known and the home they now must go visit. Oftentimes the economics of keeping a large family home make little sense after a divorce. Carefully consider and be open to all options.

11.7 How do I determine how much our house is worth?

In a divorce, the value of your home can be determined a number of ways. You and your spouse can agree to the value of your home. You can seek advice from a local real estate agent on the approximate value of your home through a market analysis. Or, for a more authoritative valuation, you can hire a professional real estate appraiser to determine the value of your home. Talk to your attorney to determine the best method to value your home in your divorce.

11.8 My house is worth less than what is owed. What are my options?

Talk with your lawyer and consider consulting with a mortgage specialist. It is important to get an accurate assessment of the value of your house. Consider working with a professional, such as an appraiser or realtor, to obtain the estimated fair market value of your home.

If your house is "underwater," meaning, you owe more on the mortgage than your house is worth, you may decide to list your house for sale and keep it on the market while continuing to make your mortgage payments. Another option to consider is a *short sale,* where the lender accepts less money for your house than you owe. Seek advice from your lawyer and other financial experts to determine which option is best for you.

11.9 What is meant by *equity* in my home?

Regardless of who is awarded your house, the court will consider whether the spouse not receiving the house should be compensated for the equity in the house. *Equity* is the difference between the value of the home and the amount owed in mortgages against the property.

For example, if the first mortgage is $100,000 and the second mortgage from a home equity loan is $50,000, the total debt owed against the house is $150,000. If your home is valued at $250,000, the equity in your home is $100,000. (The $250,000 value less the $150,000 debt on the property equals $100,000 in equity.)

If one of the parties remains in the home, the issue of how to give the other party his or her one-half share of the equity ($50,000) must be considered.

11.10 How will the equity in our house be divided?

If your home is going to be sold, the equity in the home will most likely be divided at the time of the sale, after the costs of the sale have been paid.

Division of Property

If either you or your spouse will be awarded the house, there are a number of options for the other party to be compensated for his or her share of the equity in the marital home. These could include:

- The spouse who does not receive the house receives other assets (for example, retirement funds) to compensate for their respective share of the equity.
- The person who remains in the home agrees to refinance the home at some future date and to pay the other party his or her share of the equity.
- The parties agree that the property be sold at a future date or upon the happening of a certain event such as the youngest child completing high school or the remarriage of the party keeping the home.

Because the residence is often among the most valuable assets considered in a divorce, it is important that you and your attorney discuss the details of its disposition. These include:

- Valuation of the property
- Refinancing to remove a party from liability for the mortgage
- The dates on which certain actions should be taken, such as listing the home for sale
- The real estate agent
- Costs for preparing the home for sale
- Making mortgage payments

If you and your spouse do not agree regarding which of you will remain in the home, the court will decide who keeps it or may order the property sold.

11.11 If my spouse signs a *quitclaim deed,* does that remove his obligation to repay the mortgage?

No. A *quitclaim deed* is a legal document that transfers one person's interest in real property to another person. However, removing his name from the title of your property will not remove his obligation to repay the mortgage.

You and your husband signed a contract with the lender to repay the debt you borrowed to purchase your home. Thus, removing your husband's name from the title on the property,does not remove his obligation to repay the mortgage. To remove your husband from the obligation, you must seek a refinance of your current mortgage. A refinancing involves obtaining a new mortgage loan to pay off the existing mortgage.

11.12 Who keeps all the household goods until the decree is signed?

The court will ordinarily not make any decisions about who keeps the household goods on a temporary basis. Most couples attempt to resolve these issues on their own rather than incur legal fees to dispute household goods on a temporary basis. However, the preliminary injunction issued at the beginning of the case prohibits either party from transferring, selling, or destroying household goods during the divorce process so that the goods remain intact and can be divided by the decree.

11.13 How can I reduce the risk that assets will be hidden, transferred, or destroyed by my spouse?

Consulting with an attorney before the filing of divorce can reduce the risk that assets will be hidden, transferred, or destroyed by your spouse. This is especially important if your spouse has a history of destroying property, incurring substantial debt, or transferring money without your knowledge.

These are among the possible actions you and your attorney can consider together:

- Placing your family heirlooms or other valuables in a safe location
- Transferring some portion of financial accounts prior to filing for divorce
- Preparing an inventory of the personal property
- Taking photographs or video of the property
- Obtaining copies of important records or statements
- Obtaining a restraining order before your spouse is served with notice of the divorce

Plans to leave the marital home should also be discussed in detail with your attorney so that any actions taken early in your case are consistent with your ultimate goals.

Speak candidly with your lawyer about your concerns so a plan can be developed that provides a level of protection that is appropriate to your circumstances.

11.14 How are assets such as cars, boats, and furniture divided and when does this happen?

In most cases spouses are able to reach their own agreements about how to divide personal property, such as household furnishings and vehicles.

If you and your spouse disagree about how to divide certain items, it can be wise to consider which items are truly valuable to you, financially or otherwise. Perhaps some of them can be easily replaced. Always look to see whether it is a good use of your attorney fees to argue over items of personal property. If a negotiated settlement cannot be reached, the issue of the division of your property will be made by the judge at trial.

11.15 How do I value our used personal property?

In a divorce, your personal property will generally be valued at its fair market value. The *fair market value* is the price a buyer would be willing to pay for the item at a garage sale or on an online auction website. For example, if you bought a sofa for $3,000 five years ago, the fair market value of the couch is what you could sell it for at a garage sale today. The fair market value is not how much the couch was when you bought it or how much it will cost to replace the couch. Instead, the value of your personal property is what you could reasonably sell it for in its current used condition.

11.16 My wife and I own a coin collection. How will our collection be valued and divided in our divorce?

If you own a unique collection, such as a gun, art, or coin collection, talk with your attorney about how to value the collection in your divorce. It may be that you will need the collection appraised by an expert who has specialized training and knowledge to determine its value. If you and your spouse cannot agree on who will keep the collection, it is possible the judge will order the collection to be sold. The judge may also order you to divide the collection between you and your spouse.

11.17 What is meant by a *property inventory* and how detailed should mine be?

A *property inventory* is a listing of the property you own. It may also include a brief description of the property. Discuss with your attorney the level of inventory detail needed to benefit your case.

Factors to consider when creating your inventory may include:

- The extent to which you anticipate you and your spouse will disagree regarding the division of your property
- Whether you anticipate a dispute regarding the value of the property either you or your spouse is retaining
- Whether you will have continued access to the property if a later inventory is needed or whether your spouse will retain control of the property
- Whether you or your spouse are likely to disagree about which items are premarital, inherited, or gifts from someone other than your spouse

In addition to creating an inventory, your attorney may request that you prepare a list of the property that you and your spouse have already divided or a list of the items you want but your spouse has not agreed to give to you.

If you do not have continued access to your property, talk to your attorney about taking photographs or obtaining access to the property to complete your inventory.

A sample Inventory of Property and Debts is included in the Appendix. This is a good place to start in trying to put together an inventory and will help your lawyer determine which items needs to be divided.

11.18 What happens to our individual checking and savings accounts during and after the divorce?

Regardless of whose name is on the account, bank accounts may be considered marital assets and may be divided by the court. Discuss with your attorney how to protect bank

164

accounts, how to retain access or obtain an accounting of these accounts, how to use these accounts while the case is pending, and the date on which financial accounts should be valued.

In addition, after the divorce is filed, if at all possible, avoid depositing newly earned funds into joint accounts. Assuming that your case ends in a divorce or legal separation, the marital community terminates retroactively to the date of service of the petition for dissolution. Accordingly, income earned after the service of the petition is separate property. Keeping your income earned in a separate account will avoid accounting issues later in the case.

11.19 How and when are liquid assets like bank accounts and stocks divided?

Generally, these assets will be divided after the court signs the decree of dissolution. However, talk with your attorney early in your case about the benefits of doing a pre-decree distribution of liquid assets. In many cases couples will agree to divide bank accounts equally at the outset of the case.

Discuss with your attorney whether dividing assets, or otherwise freezing accounts so that neither party can transfer assets out of the account, is advisable in your case. In any event you should keep an accounting of how you spend money used from a joint bank account while your divorce is in progress.

Stocks and investment accounts are ordinarily a part of the final agreement for the division of property and debts. If you and your spouse cannot agree on how your investments should be divided, the judge will make the decision at trial.

11.20 How is pet custody determined?

Pet custody is determined on a case-by-case basis. Arizona law is not well established on the matter of pet custody. Factors that courts have considered include:

- Whether the pet was acquired before marriage or after marriage?
- Who provided care for the pet?
- Who will best be able to meet the pet's needs?

Some courts have awarded the pet to one party and given the other party certain rights, such as:

- Specific periods of time to spent with the pet
- The right to care for the pet when the other person is not able to
- The right to be informed of the pet's health condition

If it is important to you to be awarded one of your family pets, discuss the matter with your attorney. It may be possible to reach a pet care agreement with your spouse that will allow you to share possession of and responsibility for your pets.

11.21   How will our property in another state be divided?

For the purposes of dividing your assets, out-of-state property is treated the same as property in Arizona. Accordingly, if the property acquired out of state would have been community property if acquired in Arizona, the property will be treated as community property.

As with property divided in Arizona, even if the property is in another state a judge can order your spouse either to turn the property over to you or to sign a deed or other document to transfer title to you.

11.22   Are all of the assets—such as property, bank accounts, and inheritances—that I had prior to my marriage still going to be mine after the divorce?

It depends. Property acquired prior to marriage is separate property and will be awarded to you. However, sometimes separate property cannot be easily traced, in which case the court has to make a determination of whether the separate property has lost its original character as such.

Discuss with your lawyer the following questions to determine if separate property acquired prior to marriage remains your separate property after the divorce:

- Can the premarital asset be clearly traced? For example, if you continue to own a vehicle that you brought into the marriage, it is likely that it will be awarded to you as your separate property. However, if you brought a vehicle into the marriage, sold it during the marriage, and spent the proceeds, it is less likely that the court will consider awarding you its value.

- Did you keep the property separate and titled in your name, or did you commingle it with marital assets? Premarital assets you kept separate may be more likely to be awarded to you.

Did the other spouse contribute to the increase in the value of the premarital asset, and can the value of that increase be proven? For example, suppose you owned a home prior to her marriage. After the marriage, the parties lived in the home, continuing to make mortgage payments. Your spouse may now seek a portion of the equity in the home

11.23   Will I get to keep my engagement ring?

If your engagement ring was given to you prior to your marriage, it will likely be considered a gift and treated as premarital property that you can keep.

11.24   What does it mean to *comingle property*?

Commingling occurs when one spouse's separate property is mixed or combined with the commingling property. Commingling by itself does not necessarily mean the property has changed from separate property to community property. The issue is whether the separate property has been so mixed that it is indistinguishable from the community property.

11.25   Can I keep gifts and inheritances I received during the marriage?

Similar rules apply to gifts and inheritances received during the marriage as apply to premarital assets, that is, assets you owned prior to the marriage.

Gifts that you and your spouse gave to each other may be treated as gifts if the intent that it was a gift is clear. Such intent may be shown by the fact that the gift was given as a birthday or anniversary gift, or was titled in your names. For gifts received from others during the marriage, such as a gift from a parent, the court will need to determine whether the gift was made to one party or to both.

Inheritances or bequests received during the marriage will be your separate property. With personal property, such as furniture or family heirlooms, this is fairly easy to distinguish.

Issues sometimes arise with respect to funds received if they have been commingled with community funds.

The following factors increase the probability that inherited funds will be easily traced and awarded to you as your separate property:

- It has been kept separate from the community assets, such as a separate account.
- It is titled in your name only.
- It can be clearly identified.
- It has not been comingled with community assets.
- Your spouse has not contributed to its care, operation, or improvement.

It is less likely that you will be awarded your full inheritance if:

- It was commingled with community assets.
- Its origin cannot be traced.
- You have placed your spouse's name on the title.
- Your spouse has contributed to the increase in the value of the inheritance.

If keeping your inheritance is important to you, talk to your attorney about the information needed to build your case.

11.26 If my spouse and I can't decide who gets what, who decides? Can that person's decision be contested?

If you and your spouse cannot agree on the division of your property, the judge will make the determination after considering the evidence at your trial.

If either party is dissatisfied with the decision reached by the judge, an appeal to a higher court is possible.

11.27 How are the values of property determined?

The value of some assets, like bank accounts, is usually not disputed. The value of other assets, such as homes or personal property, is more likely to be disputed.

If your case proceeds to trial, you may give your opinion of the value of property you own. You or your spouse may also have certain property appraised by an expert. In such cases it may be necessary to have the appraiser appear at trial to give testimony regarding the appraisal and the value of the asset.

If you own substantial assets for which the value is likely to be disputed, talk to your attorney early in your case about the benefits and costs of expert witnesses.

11.28   What does *date of valuation* mean?

Because the value of assets can go up or down while a divorce is pending, it can be necessary to determine a set date for valuing the marital assets. This is referred to as the *date of valuation*. You and your spouse can agree on the date the assets should be valued. If you cannot agree, the judge will decide the date of valuation.

Among the most common dates used are the end of the year, the date of the service of the petition for dissolution, or the date of the divorce trial.

11.29   Who gets the interest from certificates of deposit, or dividends from stock holdings during the divorce proceedings?

The interest earned on community funds in joint accounts will be awarded to both spouses. However, if separate funds (funds earned after the community terminated) are deposited into the same account, it may be necessary to determine the interest earned on community funds and the interest earned on separate funds.

11.30   Does each one of our financial accounts have to be divided in half if we agree to an equal division of our assets?

No. Rather than incurring the administrative challenges and expense of dividing each asset in half, you and your spouse can decide that one of you will take certain assets equal to the value of assets taken by the spouse. If necessary, one of you can agree to make a cash payment to the other to make an equitable division.

11.31 Is my *health savings account* an asset that can be divided in the divorce?

Yes. A *health savings account (HSA)* is a tax-advantaged medical savings account to which contributions may be made by employees, employers, or both. Your HSA is an asset to be included in the property distribution and may be divided according to your divorce decree and transferred to another HSA. A division according to a decree does not constitute a distribution and is a tax-free transfer.

11.32 I worked very hard for years to support my family while my spouse completed an advanced degree. Do I have a right to any of my spouse's future earnings?

Your contributions during the marriage are a factor to be considered in any award of spousal maintenance. Be sure to give your attorney a complete history of your contributions to the marriage and ask about their impact on the outcome of your case.

In addition, if your spouse is a professional (lawyer, doctor, accountant), your spouse may have developed professional goodwill during the marriage, which can be valued and divided as a marital asset. Talk to your lawyer about the possibility of valuing your spouse's goodwill and how that affects your case.

11.33 My spouse owns a business. Am I entitled to a share of my spouse's business?

Many factors determine whether you will be entitled to a share of your spouse's business and in what form you might receive it. If the business was established during the marriage, even if you do not work in the business, the business is considered a community business. Community businesses should be valued by an expert.

Even if your spouse is keeping the business, you should be entitled to your community share (one-half the value) of the business.

If your spouse owned the business prior to the marriage, it is still possible for you to obtain a share of the business. Discuss with your lawyer the following:

- Your role, if any, in operating the business or increasing its value

- The amount withdrawn from the business for use by the community
- Whether the business retained earnings in order to build the business
- Whether the community contributed funds to the business

If you or your husband owns a business, it is important that you work with your attorney early in your case to develop a strategy for valuing the business and making your case for how it should be treated in the division of property and debts.

11.34 My husband and I have owned and run our own business together for many years. Can I be forced out of it?

Deciding what should happen with a family business when divorce occurs can be a challenge. Because of the risk for future conflict between you and your spouse, the value of the business is likely to be substantially decreased if you both remain owners.

In discussing your options with your lawyer, consider the following questions:

- If one spouse retains ownership of the business, are there enough other assets for the other spouse to receive a fair share of the total community assets?
- Which spouse has the skills and experience to continue running the business?
- What would you do if you weren't working in the business?
- What is the value of the business?
- What is the market for the business if it were to be sold?
- Could you remain an employee of the business for some period of time even if you were not an owner?

You and your spouse know your business best. With the help of your lawyers, you may be able to create a settlement that can satisfy you both. If not, the judge will make the decision for you at trial.

11.35 I suspect my spouse is hiding assets, but I can't prove it. How can I protect myself if I discover later that I was right?

Ask your lawyer to include language in your divorce decree to address your concern. Insist that it include an acknowledgment by your spouse that the agreement was based upon a full and complete disclosure of your spouse's financial condition. Discuss with your lawyer a provision that allows for setting aside the agreement if it is later discovered that assets were hidden.

11.36 My spouse says I'm not entitled to a share of his stock options because he gets to keep them only if he stays employed with his company. What are my rights?

Stock options are often a very valuable asset. They are also one of the most complex issues when dividing assets during a divorce for these, among other, reasons:

- Each company has its own rules about awarding and exercising stock options.
- Complete information is needed from the employer.
- There are different methods for calculating the value of stock options.
- The reasons the options were given can impact the valuation and division. For example, some are given for future performance and may be considered separate property.
- There are cost and tax considerations when options are exercised.

Rather than being awarded a portion of the stock options themselves, you are likely to receive a share of the proceeds when the stock options are exercised.

If either you or your spouse owns stock options, begin discussing this asset with your attorney early in your case to allow sufficient time to settle the issues or to be well prepared for trial.

11.37 What is a *premarital agreement* and how might it affect the property settlement phase of the divorce?

A *premarital agreement,* sometimes referred to as a *prenuptial* or *antenuptial agreement,* is a contract entered into between two people prior to their marriage. It can include provisions for how assets and debts will be divided in the event the marriage is terminated, as well as provisions regarding spousal maintenance.

Your property settlement is likely to be impacted by the terms of your premarital agreement if the agreement is upheld as valid by the court.

11.38 Can a prenuptial agreement be contested during the divorce?

Yes. The court may consider many factors in determining whether to uphold your premarital agreement. Among them are:

- Whether your agreement was entered into voluntarily
- Whether your agreement was fair and reasonable at the time it was signed
- Whether you and your spouse gave a complete disclosure of your assets and debts when it was signed
- Whether you and your spouse each had your own lawyer
- Whether you and your spouse each had enough time to consider the agreement

If you have a premarital agreement, bring a copy of it to the initial consultation with your attorney. Be sure to provide your lawyer with a detailed history of the facts and circumstances surrounding reaching and signing the agreement.

11.39 I'm Jewish and want my husband to cooperate with obtaining a *get cooperation clause,* which is a divorce document under our religion. Can I get a court order for this?

Talk to your lawyer about obtaining a *get cooperation clause* in your divorce decree, including a provision regarding who should pay for it.

11.40 Who will get the frozen embryo of my egg and my spouse's sperm that we have stored at the health clinic?

The law on this issue is not yet established in Arizona. The terms of your contract with the clinic may impact the rights you and your spouse may have to the embryo, so provide a copy of it to your attorney for review.

11.41 Will debts be considered when determining the division of the property?

Yes. The court will consider any debts incurred during the course of the marriage when dividing the property. For example, if you are awarded a car valued at $12,000, but you owe a $10,000 debt on the same vehicle, the court will take that debt into consideration in the overall division of the assets. Similarly, if one spouse agrees to pay substantial community credit card debt, this obligation may also be considered in the final determination of the division of property and debts.

If your spouse incurred debts that you believe should be his or her sole responsibility, tell your attorney. Some debts may be considered noncommunity and treated separately from other debts incurred during the marriage. For example, if your spouse spent large sums of money on gambling or illegal drugs without your knowledge, you may be able to argue that those debts should be the sole responsibility of your spouse.

11.42 What is a *property settlement agreement*?

A *property settlement agreement,* also referred to as a *property separation agreement,* is a written document that includes all of the financial agreements you and your spouse have reached in your divorce. This may include the division of property, debts, child support, spousal maintenance, insurance, and attorney fees.

The property settlement may be a separate document, or it may be incorporated into the decree of dissolution, which is the final court order dissolving your marriage.

11.43 What happens after my spouse and I approve the property settlement agreement? Do we still have to go to court?

Not necessarily. After you and your spouse approve and sign the property settlement agreement or decree, it must still be approved by your judge. In most counties, the property settlement agreement and consent decree will be submitted to the court. The judge will then review the documents, and if the judge approves the document the consent decree will be signed. Upon the judge filing the consent decree with the clerk of the court, your divorce is considered final and all trial dates will be vacated (canceled).

In some counties, if you prefer you may be able to schedule a hearing with the judge to have your consent decree entered by the court at the hearing. The judge will go over the terms of the consent decree with each party, and after the judge is assured that this is the final agreement and that both parties believe it to be fair under the circumstances, the judge may sign the consent decree at the final hearing. A final hearing can be scheduled after the passing of the sixty-day mandatory waiting period under Arizona law, assuming you and your spouse have also resolved all matters pertaining to your minor children.

In most cases, so long as the sixty-day period has elapsed and there are no other pending issues, you simply submit your decree to the judge for approval and neither you or your spouse have to go to court.

11.44 If my spouse and I think our property settlement agreement is fair, why does the judge have to approve it?

The judge has a duty to ensure that all property settlement agreements in divorces are fair, reasonable, and equitable under Arizona law. For this reason, your judge must review your agreement. The judge can consider the facts and circumstances of your case when reviewing the agreement.

11.45 What happens to the property distribution if one of us dies before the divorce proceedings are completed?

If your spouse dies prior to your divorce decree being entered, you will be considered married and treated as a surviving spouse under the law. Discuss with your lawyer the benefits of making an estate plan or modifying your estate plan prior to filing your divorce.

11.46 After our divorce is final, can the property agreement be modified?

Property division is different than parenting time and child support, which are always modifiable, and spousal maintenance, which may be modified.

Generally, provisions in your property settlement agreement or decree concerning the distribution of your assets and debts are not modifiable. Absent an uncommon instance of fraud, duress, or newly discovered evidence, the judge will not entertain a modification of a property settlement agreement.

If both parties agree to revise or modify portions of the property settlement agreement, then talk with your attorney about filing a stipulation to amend the property settlement agreement.

12

Benefits: Insurance, Retirement, and Pensions

During your marriage, you might have taken certain employment benefits for granted. You might not have given much thought each month to having health insurance through your spouse's work. When you find yourself in a divorce, suddenly these benefits come to the forefront of your mind.

You might also, even unconsciously, have seen your own employment retirement benefits as belonging to you and not to your spouse and referred to "my 401(k)" or "my pension." After all, you are the one who went to work every day to earn it, right?

When you divorce, some benefits arising from your spouse's employment will end, some may continue for a period of time, and others may be divided between you. Retirement funds, in particular, are often one of the valuable marital assets to be divided in a divorce.

Whether the benefits are from your employer or from your spouse's, with your attorney's help you will develop a better understanding of which benefits the law considers to be "yours," "mine," and "ours" for continuing or dividing.

12.1 Will my children continue to have health coverage through my spouse's work even though we're divorcing?

If either you or your spouse currently provides health insurance for your children, the court will order the insurance to remain in place until each child reaches the age of majority or for long as it remains available and support is being paid for your child.

The cost of insurance for the children will be taken into consideration in determining the amount of child support to be paid.

12.2 Will I continue to have health insurance through my spouse's work after the divorce?

No. After the divorce you are required to obtain your own health insurance. You may obtain different insurance, or in some cases you may remain with the same insurance you had through your spouse's employment. This is referred to as *COBRA coverage*. *COBRA* is available under federal law for a period of up to thirty-six months.

Investigate the cost of continuing on your spouse's employer-provided plans under *COBRA* after the expiration of your previous coverage. Although coverage may be able to be maintained, the cost can be very high, so you will want to determine whether it's a realistic option.

In some cases, it may be possible to stay on your spouse's insurance if you are legally separated as opposed to divorced. If health insurance is important to you and neither party is planning on remarrying in the near future, talk to your lawyer about this option. Whether this option is available depends on your spouse's health insurance plan.

Begin early to investigate your eligibility for coverage on your spouse's health insurance plan after the entry of the decree and your options for your future health insurance. The cost of your health care is an important factor when pursuing spousal support and planning your postdivorce budget.

12.3 What is a *qualified domestic relations order*?

A *qualified domestic relations order (QDRO)* is a court order that requires a retirement or pension plan administrator to pay you the share of your former spouse's retirement that was awarded to you in the decree. The order helps ensure that a nonemployee spouse receives his or her share directly from the employee spouse's plan.

Obtaining a QDRO is a critical step in the divorce process. They can be complex documents, and a number of steps are required to reduce future concerns about enforcement and to fully protect your rights. These court orders must comply with numerous technical rules and be approved by the plan administrator, who may be located outside of Arizona.

Whenever possible, court orders dividing retirement plans should be entered at the same time as the decree of dissolution.

12.4 How many years must I have been married before I'm eligible to receive a part of my spouse's retirement fund or pension?

To be eligible to receive a part of your spouse's retirement or pension fund, some portion of the retirement or pension must be earned during the marriage. Thus, even if your marriage is not of long duration, you may be entitled to a portion of your spouse's retirement fund or pension accumulated during the marriage. For example, if you were married for three years and your spouse contributed $10,000 to a 401(k) plan during the marriage, the $10,000 is considered community property. You are eligible to receive one-half of the community portion of the 401(k), taking into consideration all gains and losses at the time of distribution, when dividing your property and debts.

12.5 I contributed to my pension plan for ten years before I got married. Will my spouse get half of my entire pension?

No. Your spouse is entitled to only one-half of the portion of your retirement that was acquired during the marriage.

If either you or your spouse made premarital contributions to a pension or retirement plan, be sure to let your attorney know. This is information essential to determine which portion of the retirement plan should be treated as "premarital" and thus unlikely to be shared.

12.6 I plan to keep my same job after my divorce. Will my former spouse get half of the money I contribute to my retirement plan after my divorce?

No. Your former spouse is entitled only to that portion of your retirement accumulated during the marriage.

Talk with your attorney so that the language of the court order ensures protection of your postdivorce retirement contributions.

12.7 Am I still entitled to a share of my spouse's retirement even though I never contributed to one during our twenty-five-year marriage?

Yes. Retirements are often the most valuable asset accumulated during a marriage. Consequently, your judge will consider the retirement along with all of the other marital assets and debts when dividing property.

12.8 My lawyer says I'm entitled to a share of my spouse's retirement. How can I find out how much I get and when I'm eligible to receive it?

More than one factor will determine your rights to collect from your spouse's retirement. One factor will be the terms of the court order dividing the retirement. The court order will tell you whether you are entitled to a set dollar amount, a percentage, or a fraction to be determined based upon the length of your marriage and how long your spouse continues working. For a defined benefit plan, such as a pension, the fraction used by the court to determine how much you are eligible to receive will be the number of years you were married while your spouse was employed at that company divided by the total number of years your spouse is employed with the company.

Another factor will be the terms of the retirement plan itself. Some provide for lump sum withdrawals; others issue payments in monthly installments. Review the terms of your court order and contact the plan administrator to obtain the clearest understanding of your rights and benefits.

12.9 If I am eligible to receive my spouse's retirement benefits, when am I eligible to begin collecting them? Do I have to be sixty-five to collect them?

It depends upon the terms of your spouse's retirement plan. In some cases, as in the case of private employer plans, it is possible to begin receiving your share at the earliest date your spouse is eligible to receive them, regardless of whether he or she elects to do so.

In other cases, such as government plans, it is likely you cannot receive your share until your spouse elects to receive his or her share. Check the terms of your spouse's plan to learn your options.

12.10 What happens if my former spouse is old enough to receive benefits but I'm not?

Ordinarily you will be eligible to begin receiving your share of the benefits when your former spouse begins receiving his or hers. Depending upon the plan, you may be eligible to receive them sooner.

12.11 Am I entitled to *cost-of-living increases* on my share of my spouse's retirement?

It depends. If your spouse has a retirement plan that includes a provision for a *cost-of-living allowance (COLA),* talk to your lawyer about whether this can be included in the court order dividing the retirement.

In choosing a lawyer, consider one who has familiarity with pension and retirement plans so that you can ensure your decree is worded correctly. Plans generally have a number of rights, such as COLA increases, ability to take loans, survivor and widow's benefits. These are valuable rights that you could potentially lose if your divorce decree does not include designation of all these rights and benefits.

12.12 What circumstances might prevent me from receiving part of my spouse's retirement benefits?

Some government pension plans, if they are in lieu of a Social Security benefit, are not subject to division. If you or your spouse is employed by a government agency, talk with your lawyer about whether you are entitled to any other retirement benefits and how this may affect the property settlement in your case.

12.13 Does the death of my spouse affect the pay-out of retirement benefits to me or to our children?

It depends upon both the nature of your spouse's retirement plan and the terms of the court order dividing the retirement. If you want to be eligible for survivorship benefits from your spouse's pension, discuss the issue with your attorney before your case is settled or goes to trial. He or she can advise you.

Some plans allow only a surviving spouse or former spouse to be a beneficiary. Others may allow for the naming of an alternate beneficiary, such as your children.

12.14 Can I still collect on my former spouse's Social Security benefits if he or she passes on before I do?

It depends. You may be eligible to receive benefits if:

- You were married to your spouse for ten or more years
- You are not remarried
- You are at least sixty-two years old
- The benefit you would receive based on your own earning record is less than the benefit you would receive from your former spouse

For more information, contact your local Social Security Administration office or visit the SSA website at (www.ssa.gov).

12.15 What orders might the court enter regarding life insurance?

The judge may order you or your spouse to maintain a life insurance policy to ensure that future support payments, such as child support and spousal maintenance, are made. In most cases you will be required to pay for your own life insurance after your divorce, and you should include this as an expense in your monthly budget.

12.16 Because we share children, should I consider my spouse as a beneficiary on my life insurance?

It depends upon your intentions. If your intention is to give the money to your former spouse, by all means name the other parent as beneficiary.

However, if you intend the life insurance proceeds to be used for the benefit of your children, talk with your attorney about your options. You may consider naming a trustee to manage the life insurance proceeds on behalf of your children, and there may be reasons to choose someone other than your former spouse.

12.17 Can the court require in the decree that I be the beneficiary of my spouse's insurance policy, for as long as the children are minors or indefinitely?

When a court order is entered for life insurance, it is ordinarily for the purpose of ensuring payment of future support and will terminate when the support obligation has ended. Naming you as the beneficiary on your spouse's insurance policy for the purpose of ensuring payment of future child support is one option. The court may also name the children directly as beneficiaries or require a trust be established to receive the life insurance proceeds on behalf of your children.

12.18 My spouse is in the military. What are my rights to benefits after the divorce?

As the former spouse of a military member, the types of benefits to which you may be entitled are typically determined by the number of years you were married, the number of years your spouse was in the military while you were married, and whether you have remarried. Be sure you obtain accurate information about these dates.

Among the benefits for which you may be eligible are:

- A portion of your spouse's military retirement pay
- A survivor benefit in the event of your spouse's death
- Health care or participation in a temporary, transitional health care program
- Ability to keep your military identification card
- Use of certain military facilities, such as the commissary

183

Although your divorce is pending, educate yourself about your right to future military benefits so that you can plan for your future with clarity. If your divorce is still pending, contact your base legal office, or for more information, visit the website for the branch of the military of which your spouse was a member.

13

Division of Debts

Throughout a marriage, most couples will have disagreements about money from time to time. You might think extra money should be spent on a family vacation, but your spouse might insist it should be saved for your retirement. You might think it's time to finally buy a new car, but your spouse thinks you driving the ten-year-old van for two more years is a better idea.

If you and your spouse had different philosophies about saving and spending during your marriage, chances are you will have some differing opinions when dividing your debts in divorce. What you both can count on is that Arizona law provides that, to reach a fair outcome, the payment of debts must also be taken into consideration when dividing the assets from your marriage. Just like community assets are divided, community liabilities also must be divided.

There are steps you can take to ensure the best outcome possible when it comes to dividing your community debt. These include providing accurate and complete debt information to your lawyer and asking your lawyer to include provisions in your divorce decree to protect you in the future if your spouse refuses to pay his or her share.

Although it is much easier to divide assets than to divide debt, both must occur to receive a fair result. Regardless of the division of debts from your marriage, know that you will gradually build your independent financial success when making a fresh start after your divorce is final.

13.1 Who is responsible for paying credit card bills and making house payments during the divorce proceedings?

Work with your attorney and your spouse to reach a temporary agreement on the payment of community debt. Discuss the importance of making at least minimum payments on time to avoid substantial finance charges and late fees.

If an agreement cannot be reached with your spouse, it may be possible to file for temporary orders so that the court, on a temporary basis, can order how these debts will be paid.

Oftentimes the spouse who remains in the home will be responsible for the mortgage payments, taxes, utilities, and most other ordinary expenses.

If you are concerned that you cannot afford to stay in the marital home on a temporary basis, talk with your attorney about your options prior to your temporary orders hearing.

13.2 What, if anything, should I be doing with the credit card companies as we go through the divorce?

If possible, it is best to obtain some separate credit prior to the divorce. This will help you establish credit in your own name and help you with necessary purchases following a separation.

Begin by obtaining a copy of your credit report from at least two of the three nationwide consumer reporting companies: Experian, Equifax, or TransUnion. *The Fair Credit Reporting Act* entitles you to a free copy of your credit report from each of these three companies every twelve months. To order your free annual report online, go to (www.annualcreditreport.com), call toll-free to (877) 322-8228, or complete an Annual Credit Report Request Form and mail it to: Annual Credit Report Request Service, P.O. Box 105281, Atlanta, Georgia 30348-5281.

Your spouse may have incurred debt using your name. This information is important to relay to your attorney. If you and your spouse have joint credit card accounts, contact the credit card companies to see if you can close the account. Generally, the account cannot be closed if there is a balance due. However, it may be possible to decrease the credit limit so that additional debt cannot be incurred.

If your spouse is an authorized user on any of your accounts, it may be possible to remove your spouse from the account.

If you want to maintain credit with a company, ask to have a new account in your own name. Be sure to let your spouse know if you close an account he or she has been using.

13.3   How is credit card debt divided?

Credit card debt incurred during the marriage is a community obligation. Accordingly, absent unusual circumstances, the debt will be divided in half. It will be divided as a part of the overall division of the marital property and debts. Just as in the division of property, the parties may decide to adjust the obligation to pay the debt as part of the overall settlement and equalization of property.

If your spouse has exclusively used a credit card for purposes that did not benefit the family, such as gambling, talk with your attorney. In most cases the court will not review a lengthy history of how you and your spouse used the credit cards, but there can be exceptions.

13.4   Am I responsible for repayment of my spouse's student loans?

It depends. If your spouse incurred student loans prior to the marriage, it is most likely that he or she will be ordered to pay that debt.

If the debt was incurred during the marriage, how the funds were used may have an impact on who is ordered to pay them. For example, if your spouse borrowed $3,000 during the marriage for tuition, your spouse may be ordered to pay that debt. However, if a $3,000 student loan was taken out by your spouse, but $1,000 of it was used for a family vacation, then the court would be more likely to order the debt shared.

The court may also consider payment on student loan debt when calculating spousal maintenance.

If you were a joint borrower on your spouse's student loan and your spouse fails to pay the loan, the lender may attempt to collect from you even if your spouse has been ordered to pay the debt.

If either you or your spouse has student loan debt, be sure to give your attorney the complete history regarding the debt and ask about the most likely outcome under the facts of your case.

13.5 During the divorce proceedings, am I still responsible for debt my spouse continues to accrue?

It depends. Although the debts incurred by your spouse after service of the petition for dissolution of marriage are your spouse's separate obligations, you may still be responsible to the credit card company. So, although the court can order your spouse to pay, if your spouse does not pay, the credit card company may still come after you on credit cards that are in your name.

Be sure to discuss with your lawyer protection of your rights to assert claims against your spouse in the event your spouse does not pay for his or her separate debts after the filing of the petition for dissolution of marriage.

13.6 During the marriage my spouse applied for and received several credit cards without my knowledge. Am I responsible for them?

Unfortunately, yes. During a marriage, both parties have equal management and control over property and the right to incur debt except under specific exceptions. Accordingly, the debt acquired during the marriage is considered community debt and generally equally divided at the time of division of assets and liabilities.

13.7 During our marriage, we paid off thousands of dollars of debt incurred by my spouse before we were married. Will the court take this into consideration when dividing our property and debt?

It depends on how the payment of the premarital debt is characterized. If it was a loan that was intended to be paid back to the community by your spouse at some point, this may be a factor to consider. However, if there was no agreement, then the payment of the separate debt will likely be considered a gift of community property to separate obligations. Be sure to let your attorney know if either you or your spouse brought substantial debt into the marriage.

13.8 Regarding debts, what is a *hold harmless clause,* and why should it be in the divorce decree?

A *hold harmless provision* is intended to protect you in the event that your spouse fails to follow a court order to pay a debt after the divorce is granted. The language typically provides that your spouse shall "indemnify and hold [you] harmless from liability" on the debt.

If you and your spouse have a joint debt and your spouse fails to pay, the creditor may nevertheless attempt to collect from you. This is because the court is without power to change the creditor's rights and can make orders affecting only you and your spouse.

In the event your spouse fails to pay a court-ordered debt and the creditor attempts collection from you, the hold harmless provision in your divorce decree can be used in an effort to insist that payment is made by your former spouse.

13.9 Why do my former spouse's doctors say they have a legal right to collect from me when my former spouse was ordered to pay her own medical bills?

Your divorce decree does not take away the legal rights of creditors to collect debts. Contact your attorney about your rights to enforce the court order that your spouse pay his or her own medical bills.

13.10 My spouse and I have agreed that I will keep our home. Why must I refinance the mortgage?

There may be a number of reasons why your spouse is asking you to refinance the mortgage. First, the mortgage company cannot be forced to take your spouse's name off of the mortgage note. This means that if you did not make the house payments, the lender could pursue collection against your spouse.

Second, your spouse may want to receive their share of the home equity. It may be possible for you to borrow additional money at the time of refinancing to pay your spouse his or her share of the equity in the home.

Third, the mortgage on your family home may prevent your spouse from buying a home in the future. Because there remains a risk that your spouse could be pursued for the debt to the mortgage company, it is unlikely that a second lender will want to take the risk of extending further credit to your spouse.

13.11   Can I file for bankruptcy while my divorce is pending?

Yes. Consult with your attorney if you are considering filing for bankruptcy while your divorce is pending. It will be important for you to ask yourself a number of questions, such as:

- Should I file for bankruptcy on my own or with my spouse?
- How will filing for bankruptcy affect my ability to purchase a home in the future?
- Which debts can be discharged in bankruptcy, and which cannot?
- How will a bankruptcy affect the division of property and debts in the divorce?
- How might a delay in the divorce proceeding due to a bankruptcy impact my case?
- What form of bankruptcy is best for my situation?

If you use a different attorney for your bankruptcy than you have for your divorce, be sure that each attorney is kept fully informed about the developments in the other case.

13.12   What happens if my spouse files for bankruptcy during our divorce?

Contact your attorney right away. The filing of a bankruptcy while your divorce is pending can have a significant impact on your divorce. Your attorney can advise you whether certain debts are likely to be discharged in the bankruptcy, the delay a bankruptcy may cause to your divorce, and whether bankruptcy is an appropriate option for you.

13.13   Can I file for divorce while I am in bankruptcy?

Yes, however, you must receive the bankruptcy court's permission to proceed with the divorce because in a bankruptcy your property is protected from debt collection by the *automatic stay*. The stay can also prevent the divorce court from dividing property between you and your spouse until you obtain the bankruptcy court's permission to proceed with the divorce.

13.14 What should I do if my former spouse files for bankruptcy after our divorce?

Contact your attorney immediately. If you learn that your former spouse has filed for bankruptcy, you may have certain rights to object to the discharge of any debts your spouse was ordered to pay under your divorce decree. If you fail to take action, it is possible that you will be held responsible for debts your spouse was ordered to pay.

13.15 If I am awarded child support or spousal maintenance in my decree, can these obligations be discharged if my former spouse files for bankruptcy after our divorce?

No, support obligations such as child support and spousal maintenance are not dischargeable in bankruptcy, meaning these debts cannot be eliminated in a bankruptcy proceeding.

13.16 What happens if my former spouse does not pay their obligations in the decree?

If your former spouse does not pay the debts assigned to him or her in the decree, talk to your attorney about how to enforce the obligation. A party is in contempt of court if they willfully disobey or disregard a court order. Talk with your attorney to determine whether a *contempt of court* action may be filed in your case to enforce your rights under your decree.

14

Taxes

Nobody likes a surprise letter from the Internal Revenue Service saying he or she owes more taxes. When your divorce is over, you want to be sure that you don't later discover you owe taxes you weren't expecting to pay.

A number of tax issues may arise in your divorce. Your attorney may not be able to answer all of your tax questions, so consulting your accountant or tax advisor for additional advice might be necessary.

Taxes are important considerations in both settlement negotiations and trial preparation. They should not be overlooked. Taxes can impact many of your decisions, including those regarding spousal maintenance, division of property, and the receipt of benefits.

Be sure to ask the professionals helping you about the tax implications in your divorce so you don't get a letter in the mail that begins, "Dear Taxpayer:...."

14.1 Will either my spouse or I have to pay income tax when we transfer property or pay a property settlement to each other according to our divorce decree?

No. However, it is important that you see the future tax consequences of a subsequent withdrawal, sale, or transfer of certain assets you receive in your divorce. The tax basis of property still exists. Accordingly, you may have to pay taxes upon the sale of any property.

It is important to ask your attorney to take tax consequences into consideration when looking at the division of your assets.

14.2   Is the amount of child support I pay tax deductible?
No.

14.3   Do I have to pay income tax on any child support I receive?
No. Your child support is tax free regardless of when it is paid or when it is received.

14.4   What does the IRS consider spousal maintenance (alimony)?
Amounts paid under a divorce decree or according to a written separation agreement entered into between you and your spouse will be considered spousal maintenance if:

- You and your spouse or former spouse do not file a joint return with each other
- The payment is in cash (including checks or money orders)
- The payment is received by (or on behalf of) your spouse or former spouse
- You and your former spouse are not members of the same household when you make the payment
- You have no liability to make the payment (in cash or property) after the death of your spouse or former spouse
- Your payment is not treated as child support or a property settlement

Thus, not all payments made according to a divorce or separation decree are spousal maintenance.

Spousal maintenance does not include:

- Child support
- Noncash property settlements
- Payments to keep up the payer's property
- Use of the payer's property

14.5   Is the amount of spousal maintenance I am ordered to pay tax deductible?

Not if the agreement was entered into after January 1, 2019. Spousal support paid according to a court order prior to December 31, 2018, is tax deductible. This will include court-ordered spousal maintenance and may also include other forms of support provided to your former spouse (but not child support). The fact that your payments are not deductible is a factor to consider when determining a fair amount of spousal maintenance to be paid in your case.

14.6   Do I have to pay tax on the spousal maintenance I receive?

No. If your order for spousal maintenance was entered after January 1, 2019, you do not pay income tax on the spousal maintenance you receive. If your order was entered prior to January 1, 2019, then the spousal maintenance payment will need to be included in your income. Child support payments to you are not included in your income regardless if the order was before or after January 1, 2019.

Tax laws change. Be sure to consult with your tax advisor about any changes to the tax law. If you are paying tax on your spousal maintenance, then you may need to make estimated quarterly tax payments throughout the year. Talking to a tax advisor is important.

14.7   During the divorce proceedings, is our tax filing status affected?

It can be. You are considered unmarried if your decree is final by December 31 of the tax year. Under Arizona law, your decree becomes final when the decree is filed with the clerk of the court after it is signed by the judge.

If you and your spouse have entered into a property settlement agreement close to the end of the calendar year, you may wish to consider not lodging the consent decree until after the first of the year. This way you can still file jointly because your divorce was not considered final on December 31. Generally, there are significant tax benefits to filing jointly. Discuss this option with your attorney and tax advisor.

Taxes

If you are considered unmarried, your filing status is either "single" or, under certain circumstances, "head of household." If your decree is not final as of December 31, your filing status is either "married filing a joint return" or "married filing a separate return," unless you live apart from your spouse and meet the exception for "head of household."

While your divorce is in progress, talk to both your tax advisor and your attorney about your filing status. It may be beneficial to figure your tax on both a joint return and a separate return to see which gives you the lower tax. IRS Publication 504, Divorced or Separated Individuals, provides more detail on tax issues while you are going through a divorce. For more information go to (www.irs.gov/pub/irs-pdf/p504.pdf).

14.8   Should I file a joint income tax return with my spouse while our divorce is pending?

Consult your tax advisor to determine the risks and benefits of filing a joint return with your spouse. Compare this with the consequences of filing your tax return separately. Often the overall tax liability will be less with the filing of a joint return, but other factors are important to consider.

When deciding whether to file a joint return with your spouse, consider any concerns you have about the accuracy and truthfulness of the information on the tax return. If you have any doubts, consult both your attorney and your tax advisor before agreeing to sign a joint tax return with your spouse. Prior to filing a return with your spouse, try to reach agreement about how any tax owed or refund expected will be shared, and ask your lawyer to assist you in getting this in writing.

14.9   My spouse will not cooperate in providing the necessary documents to prepare or file our taxes jointly. What options do I have?

Talk with your attorney about requesting your spouse cooperate in the preparation and filing of your joint return. Although a judge cannot order your spouse to sign a joint return, he or she can penalize them for their unreasonable refusal to do so.

14.10 For tax purposes, is one time of year better to divorce than another?

It depends upon your tax situation. If you and your spouse agree that it would be beneficial to file joint tax returns for the year in which you are divorcing, you may wish to not have your divorce finalized before the end of the year. Your marital status for filing income taxes is determined by your status on December 31. Consequently, if you both want to preserve your right to file a joint return, your decree should not be entered before December 1 of that year.

14.11 What tax consequences should I consider regarding the sale of our home?

When your home is sold, whether during your divorce or after, the sale may be subject to a *capital gains tax*. If your home was your primary residence and you lived in the home for two of the preceding five years, you may be eligible to exclude up to $250,000 of the gain on the sale of your home. If both you and your spouse meet the ownership and residence tests, you may be eligible to exclude up to $500,000 of the gain.

If you anticipate the gain on the sale of your residence to be over $250,000, talk with your attorney early in the divorce process about a plan to minimize the tax liability. For more information, *see* IRS Publication 523, Selling Your Home at (www.irs.gov/pub/irs-pdf/p523.pdf).

14.12 How might capital gains tax be a problem for me years after the divorce?

Future capital gains tax on the sale of property should be discussed with your attorney during the negotiation and trial preparation stages of your case. This is especially important if the sale of the property is imminent. Failure to do so may result in an unfair outcome.

For example, suppose you agree that your spouse will be awarded the proceeds from the sale of your home valued at $200,000, after the real estate commission, and you will take the stock portfolio also valued at $200,000.

Suppose that after the divorce, you decide to sell the stock. It is still valued at $200,000, but you learn that its original price was $120,000 and that you must pay capital gains tax of

15 percent on the $80,000 of gain. You pay tax of $12,000, leaving you with $188,000.

Meanwhile, your former spouse sells the marital home but pays no capital gains tax because he qualifies for the $250,000 exemption. He is left with the full $200,000.

Tax implications of your property division should always be discussed with your attorney, with support from your tax advisor as needed.

14.13 During and after the divorce, who gets to claim the children as dependents?

Where child support has been ordered according to the Arizona Child Support Guidelines, the exemptions will be determined according to the work sheet prepared. However, you and your spouse may agree to a different arrangement. For example, if there are two children, you may each agree to take one child as a dependency exemption. Additionally, if one party has income so low or so high that he or she will not benefit from the dependency exemption, you may want to agree to award the exemption to the other parent.

If a party is paying child support and is entitled to the dependency exemption, the obligor must be current on child support by December 31 in order to claim the exemption.

14.14 My decree says I have to sign IRS Form 8332 so my former spouse can claim our child as an exemption, because I am the primary parent. Should I sign it once for all future years?

No. Parenting time and child support can be modified in the future. If there is a future modification of parenting time or support, which parent is entitled to claim your child as an exemption could change. The best practice is to provide your former spouse a copy of Form 8332 signed by you for the appropriate tax year only.

14.15 Who is entitled to the child-care tax credit?

The federal income tax credit for child care is already factored into the Arizona Child Support work sheet depending on who pays for child care. The credit will be considered in determining child support.

The value of the federal child-care tax credit must be subtracted from the actual costs of child care to arrive at a figure for net child-care expenses owed by the spouse paying support.

14.16 Do I have to pay taxes on the portion of my spouse's 401(k) that was awarded to me in the divorce?

If you have been awarded a portion of your former spouse's 401(k) or 403(b) retirement plan, you are not taxed when your share of the funds are rolled over to your own individual retirement account, but when you do eventually withdraw these funds, you will be subject to regular income tax. However, it may be possible for you to elect to receive all or a portion of these assets without incurring the 10 percent early withdrawal penalty (applicable if you are under age fifty-nine and one-half) if you decide to take the money rather than keeping an account in your name or rolling over the assets to an IRA or other permitted retirement account. Talk with your attorney and your tax advisor to determine your options.

14.17 Is the cost of obtaining a divorce, including my attorney fees, tax deductible under any circumstances?

Your legal fees for obtaining a divorce are not deductible. However, because there are changes in the tax law, talk with your tax advisor regarding when and how a portion of your fees may be deductible.

You may also be able to deduct fees you pay to appraisers or accountants who help. Talk to your tax advisor about whether any portion of your attorney fees or other expenses from your divorce is deductible.

14.18 Do I have to complete a new Form W-4 for my employer because of my divorce?

Completing a new Form W-4, Employee's Withholding Certificate, will help you to claim the proper withholding allowances based upon your marital status and exemptions. Also, if you are receiving spousal maintenance, you may need to make quarterly estimated tax payments. Consult with your tax advisor to ensure you are making the most preferable tax planning decision.

14.19 What is *innocent spouse relief* and how can it help me?

Innocent spouse relief refers to a method of obtaining relief from the Internal Revenue Service for taxes owed as a result of a joint income tax return filed during your marriage. Numerous factors affect your eligibility for innocent spouse tax relief, such as:

- You would suffer a financial hardship if you were required to pay the tax.
- You did not significantly benefit from the unpaid taxes.
- You suffered abuse during your marriage.
- You thought your spouse would pay the taxes on the original return.

Talk with your attorney or your tax advisor if you are concerned about liability for taxes arising from joint tax returns filed during the marriage. You may benefit from a referral to an attorney who specializes in tax law or from working with an attorney who has other attorneys in their firm who specialize in tax issues.

15

Going to Court

For many of us, our images of going to court are created by movie scenes and our favorite television shows. We picture the witness breaking down in tears after a grueling cross-examination. We see lawyers waltzing around the courtroom, waving their arms as they plead their case to the jury.

Hollywood drama, however, is a far cry from reality. Going to court for your divorce can mean many things, ranging from a simple hearing to put the terms of your settlement on the court record to being on the witness stand giving mundane answers to questions about your monthly living expenses.

Regardless of the nature of your court proceeding, going to court often evokes a sense of anxiety. Perhaps your divorce might be the first time in your life that you have ever been in a courtroom. Be assured that these feelings of nervousness and uncertainty are normal.

Understanding what will occur in court and being well prepared for any court hearings will relieve much of your stress. Knowing the order of events, the role of the people in the courtroom, etiquette in the courtroom, and what is expected of you will make the entire experience easier.

Your lawyer will be with you at all times to support you any time you go to court. Remember, every court appearance moves you one step closer to completing your divorce so that you can move forward with the rest of your life.

15.1 What do I need to know about appearing in court and court dates in general?

Court dates are important. As soon as you receive a notice from your attorney about a court date in your case, confirm whether your attendance will be required and put it on your calendar.

Ask your attorney about the nature of the hearing, including whether the judge will be setting a trial date, listening to testimony by witnesses, or merely listening to the arguments of the lawyers. Sometimes if the court is setting dates, or the hearing is on a simple issue, the court may wish to have a telephonic hearing with the parties all appearing by telephone.

Ask whether it is necessary for you to meet with your attorney or take any other action to prepare for the hearing, such as providing additional information or documents.

Find out how long the hearing is expected to last. It may be as short as a few minutes or as long as a day or more.

If you need to attend the hearing, determine where and when to meet your attorney. Depending upon the type of hearing, your lawyer may want you to arrive in advance of the scheduled hearing time to prepare.

Make sure you know the location of the courthouse, where to park, and the floor and room number of the courtroom. Planning for such simple matters as change for a parking meter can eliminate unnecessary stress. If you want someone to go to court with you to provide support, check with your attorney first.

15.2 When and how often will I need to go to court?

Whether and how often you will need to go to court depends upon a number of factors. Depending upon the complexity of your case, whether temporary orders are sought, or whether other motions are filed, you may have only one hearing or numerous court hearings throughout the course of your divorce.

Some hearings, usually those on procedural matters, might be attended only by the attorneys or by the parties appearing telephonically. These could include requests for the other side to provide information or for the setting of certain deadlines. These hearings are often brief and sometimes are held in the judge's chambers rather than in the courtroom. Other hearings, such as temporary order hearings for parenting time or support, are attended by both parties and their attorneys.

If you and your spouse settle all of the issues in your case, the parties and their attorneys may appear in court to simply put the terms of the agreement "on the record." This means the judge will listen to the settlement, and then ask the parties if they understand the terms of the settlement and certain other questions to make sure that the agreement is fair under the circumstances. The judge will then approve the settlement as a binding agreement and ask one of the attorneys to prepare the consent decree.

If you and your spouse are not able to settle all issues in your case, then the case proceeds to trial. Your appearance will be required for the duration of the trial. In Arizona, divorce matters are heard before a judge only; juries do not hear divorces.

15.3   How much notice will I receive about appearing in court?

The amount of notice you will receive for any court hearing can vary from a few days to several weeks. Ask your attorney whether and when it will be necessary for you to appear in court on your case so that you can have ease in preparing and planning.

If you receive a notice of a hearing, contact your attorney immediately. He or she can tell you whether your appearance is required and what other steps are needed to prepare.

15.4   I am afraid to be alone in the same room with my spouse. When I go to court, is this going to happen if the lawyers go into the judge's chambers to discuss the case?

Talk to your lawyer. Prior to any court hearing, you and your spouse may be asked to wait while your attorneys meet with the judge to discuss preliminary matters.

A number of options are likely to be available to ensure that you feel safe. These might include having you or your spouse wait in different locations or having a friend or family member present.

Your lawyer wants to support you in feeling secure throughout all court proceedings. Just let him or her know your concerns.

15.5 Do I have to go to court every time there is a court hearing on any motion?

Not necessarily. Some matters will be decided by the judge after reading the papers, such as procedural motions. Other routine matters may be heard telephonically. Your lawyer will advise you which hearings you must attend.

If you have a conflict for a date that a hearing is set, let your lawyer know as soon as possible if you cannot attend. Your attorney may be able to either have your attendance excused if not necessary or will seek a continuance of the hearing.

Conflicts that arise after a hearing is set are generally not a reason to continue the hearing. Accordingly, after a hearing is set, mark your calendar so that you can be certain to attend.

15.6 My spouse's lawyer keeps asking for *continuances of court dates*. Is there anything I can do to stop this?

Continuances of court dates are not unusual in divorces. A court date might be postponed for many reasons, including a conflict on the calendar of one of the attorneys or the judge, the lack of availability of one of the parties or an important witness, or the need for more time to prepare.

Discuss with your attorney your desire to move your case forward without further delay, so that repeated requests for continuances can be resisted. Generally, the court will not allow multiple continuances unless there is good cause for a matter to be continued.

15.7 If I have to go to court, will I be put on the stand? Will there be a jury?

In Arizona, family law matters are heard before a judge only; juries do not hear divorces or other issues in family court. Whether you will be put on the stand will depend upon the nature of the issues in dispute, the judge assigned to your case, and your attorney's strategy for your case.

15.8 My lawyer said I need to be in court for our temporary orders hearing next week. What's going to happen?

A temporary orders hearing is held to determine such matters as temporary parenting time, temporary child support, temporary spousal maintenance, and other financial matters.

The procedure for your temporary hearing can vary depending upon the county in which your case was filed and the judge to which the case is assigned.

In general, the court will set a return hearing shortly after the motion for temporary orders is filed. At the return hearing the judge will determine whether there is any agreement on any of the issues on a temporary basis. The issues that are agreed to by the parties will be put on the record and made a court order. The remaining issues that need to be decided on a temporary basis will be set for a hearing, usually thirty to sixty days later. The hearing is usually no longer than one to two hours and covers narrow range of issues.

Your presence at the temporary orders hearing is important. Even though this is just a temporary arrangement, pending a final trial, the judge will hear information about your case. Often this is the first opportunity for the judge to learn about the issues in your case. In addition, the judge's ruling on temporary orders gives you a good sense of what the judge is thinking about for your case.

During the temporary orders hearing you and other witnesses might be required to take the witness stand to give testimony. Meeting with your attorney in advance to fully prepare is very important. Talk to your lawyer about the procedure you should expect for the temporary hearing in your case.

15.9 Do I have to go to court if my spouse does not respond to the petition for dissolution of marriage?

Perhaps. Even though your spouse does not file a response, you still may have to attend a default hearing to prove your case. This is generally a brief hearing in which your attorney will ask you questions relating to the issues raised in your petition, such as whether you met the jurisdictional requirements to obtain a divorce in Arizona and whether there are irreconcilable differences.

In addition, your attorney will ask you questions to prove to the judge you are entitled to the relief requested in your petition, such as the amount you have requested for spousal maintenance or child support.

At the default hearing, the judge will review and approve your divorce and may ask you several questions as well.

15.10 Are there any rules about courtroom etiquette that I need to know?

Knowing a few tips about being in the courtroom will make your experience easier.

- Dress appropriately. Avoid overly casual dress, lots of jewelry, revealing clothing, and extreme hairstyles.
- Don't bring beverages into the courtroom. Most courts have rules that do not allow food and drink in courtrooms. Generally, water is available in the courtroom.
- Dispose of chewing gum before entering the courtroom.
- Don't talk aloud in the courtroom unless you're on the witness stand or being questioned by the judge. Sometimes the courtroom has microphones that are on and therefore allow the judge or the judge's staff to hear conversations in the courtroom.
- Do not enter the judge's chambers.
- Stand up whenever the judge is entering or leaving the courtroom.
- Be sure to turn off your electronic devices.
- Be mindful that the judge may be observing you and those you bring to the hearing at all times.
- Avoid facial expressions, gestures, or the shaking or nodding of your head during the testimony of your spouse or testimony of witnesses.
- Do not bring anything up to the witness stand with you unless you ask your lawyer first.

Although you may feel anxious initially, you'll likely feel more relaxed about the courtroom setting after your hearing gets underway.

15.11 What is the role of the *bailiff*?

The *bailiff* or court clerk provides support for the judge and lawyers in the management of the court calendar and the courtroom. He or she assists in the scheduling of court hearings and the management of exhibits or legal documents given to the judge for review during the hearing.

15.12 Will there be a *court reporter,* and what will he or she do?

A *court reporter* is a professional trained to make an accurate record of the words spoken and documents offered into evidence during court proceedings. Some counties use tape recording devices rather than court reporters.

A written transcript of a court proceeding may be purchased from the court reporter. If your case is appealed, the transcript prepared by the court reporter will be used by the appeals court to review the facts of your case.

15.13 Will I be able to talk to my attorney while we are in court?

During court proceedings it is important that your attorney give his or her attention to anything being said by the judge, witnesses, or your spouse's lawyer. For this reason, your attorney will avoid talking with you when anyone else in the courtroom is speaking.

Plan to have pen and paper with you when you go to court. If your court proceeding is underway and your lawyer is listening to what is being said by others in the courtroom, write him or her a note with your questions or comments.

It is critical that your attorney hear each question asked by the other lawyer and all answers given by each witness. If not, opportunities for making objections to inappropriate evidence may be lost. You can support your attorney in doing an effective job for you by avoiding talking to him or her while a court hearing is in progress.

If your court hearing is lengthy, breaks will be taken. You can use this time to discuss with your attorney any questions or observations you have about the proceeding.

15.14 What questions might my lawyer ask me at about the problems in our marriage and why I want the divorce?

Because Arizona is a no-fault state, your lawyer will ask you questions to show the court that the marriage is irretrievably broken, without going into detail about the specific difficulties in your marriage.

The questions will be similar to these:

Attorney: Have differences arisen during the course of your marriage?

You: Yes.

Attorney: Are you aware of the services offered through conciliation services?

You: Yes.

Attorney: Do you believe that services offered through conciliation services would be helpful?

You: No.

Attorney: In your opinion, is your marriage irretrievably broken?

You: Yes.

If your spouse disagrees, he or she may give the opinion that the marriage can be saved. However, most judges recognize that it takes two willing partners for a marriage to be reconciled.

It is unlikely that you will be asked in great detail about the nature of the marital problems that led to the divorce. In the majority of cases, questions like those above will satisfy the judge that the requirements under Arizona law for the dissolving of a marriage have been met.

15.15 My lawyer said that we have to do a *pretrial statement* for my upcoming trial. What does this mean?

A *pretrial statement* is a joint statement submitted by both attorneys. This might include:

- A list of issues that have been settled
- A list of issues that are still disputed
- Agreements, referred to as *stipulations,* as to the truth of certain facts
- The names of witnesses
- Exhibits

- A summary of your position and how you want the judge to decide the case
- Any objections to exhibits or witnesses or other issues that the judge must decide

In cases in which there is no cooperation from the opposing party to do a joint pretrial statement, or where a joint pretrial statement is not feasible due to time constraints, the parties may file separate pretrial statements.

15.16 What do I need to do to assist my attorney with the pretrial statement?

Review with your lawyer the following information so your lawyer understands your position and concerns:

- The issues in dispute
- The position on the disputed issues
- The identification of witnesses
- Trial exhibits
- The status of negotiations

15.17 Besides meeting with my lawyer, is there anything else I should do to prepare for my upcoming trial?

Yes. Be sure to review your deposition and any information you provided in your discovery, such as answers to interrogatories. Also be sure to review any affidavits previously submitted to the judge, such as your affidavit of financial information that may have been prepared for your temporary hearing.

At trial, it is possible that you will be asked some of the same questions. If you think you might give different answers at trial, discuss this with your lawyer. It is important that your attorney know in advance of trial whether any information you provided during the discovery process has changed.

15.18 I'm meeting with my lawyer to prepare for trial. How do I make the most of these meetings?

Meeting with your lawyer to prepare for your trial is important to achieving a good outcome. Come to the meeting prepared to discuss the following:

- The issues in your case
- Your desired outcome on each of the issues
- The questions you might be asked at trial by both lawyers
- The exhibits that will be offered into evidence during the trial
- The witnesses for your trial
- The status of negotiations

Your meeting with your lawyer will help you better understand what to expect at your trial and make the trial experience easier.

15.19 My lawyer says that the law firm is busy with trial preparation. What exactly is my lawyer doing to prepare for my trial?

Countless tasks are necessary to perform to prepare your case for trial. These are just some of them:

- Developing arguments to be made on each of the contested issues
- Researching and reviewing the relevant law in your case
- Reviewing the facts of your case to determine which witnesses are best suited to testifying about them
- Reviewing, selecting, and preparing exhibits
- Preparing questions for all witnesses
- Preparing an opening statement
- Reviewing rules on evidence to prepare for any objections that are to made or opposed at trial
- Determining the order of witnesses and all exhibits
- Preparing your file for the day in court, including preparing a trial notebook with essential information

Your lawyer is committed to a good outcome for you in your divorce. He or she will be engaged in many important actions to fully prepare your case for trial. While at trial the efforts may seem to flow very smoothly, it is only because of the significant amount of trial preparation that is done in advance.

15.20 How do I know who my witnesses will be at trial?
Well in advance of your trial date, your lawyer will discuss with you whether other witnesses, besides you and your spouse, will be necessary. Witnesses can include family members, friends, child-care providers, or clergy members. When thinking of potential witnesses, consider your relationship with the witness, whether that witness has had an opportunity to observe relevant facts, and whether the witness has knowledge different from that of other witnesses. You may also have expert witnesses testify on your behalf. An expert witness will provide opinion testimony based upon specialized knowledge, training, or experience. For example, a psychologist, real estate appraiser, or accountant may provide expert testimony on your behalf.

15.21 My divorce is scheduled for trial. Does this mean there is no hope for a settlement?
Many cases are settled after a trial date is set. The setting of a trial date may cause you and your spouse to think about the risks and costs of going to trial. This can help you and your spouse focus on what is most important to you and lead you toward a negotiated settlement. Because the costs of preparing for and proceeding to trial are substantial, it is best to engage in settlement negotiations well in advance of your trial date. However, it is not uncommon for cases to settle a few days before trial, or even at the courthouse before your trial begins.

15.22 Can I prevent my spouse from being in the courtroom?
No. Because your spouse has a legal interest in the outcome of your divorce, he or she has a right to be present. Unless a case is sealed, Arizona courtrooms are open to the public. Consequently, it is not uncommon for persons not involved in your divorce to pass through the courtroom at various times simply because they have other business with the court.
A case is sealed in Arizona only under rare circumstances to protect the parties and their children. Accordingly, sometimes in high profile cases, to protect the privacy of the individuals and their children, a court may not allow other individuals in the courtroom or will seal parts of the record. Discuss this possibility with your attorney.

15.23 Can I take a friend or family member with me to court?

Yes. Let your attorney know in advance if you intend to bring anyone to court with you. Some people important to you may be very emotional about your divorce or your spouse. Be sure to invite someone who is better able to focus attention on supporting you rather than on his or her own feelings.

15.24 Can my friends and family be present in the courtroom during my trial?

It depends upon whether they will be witnesses in your case. In most cases where witnesses other than the husband and wife are testifying, the attorneys request that the court ask the witnesses to leave. The judge would then order all witnesses, except you and your spouse, to leave the courtroom until after they have testified.

After a witness has completed his or her testimony, he or she will ordinarily be allowed to remain in the courtroom for the remainder of the trial.

15.25 I want to do a great job testifying as a witness in my divorce trial. What are some tips?

Keep the following in mind to be a good witness on your own behalf:

- Tell the truth. Although this may not be always be comfortable, it is critical if you want your testimony to be believed by the judge.
- Listen carefully to the complete question before thinking of your answer. Wait to consider your answer until the full question is asked.
- Slow down. It's easy to speed up our speech when we are anxious. Taking your time with your answers ensures that the judge hears you and that the court reporter can accurately record your testimony.
- If you don't understand a question or don't know the answer, be sure to say so.
- If the question calls for a "yes" or "no" answer, simply say so. Then wait for the attorney to ask you the next question. If there is more you want to explain, remember that you have already told your attorney all

the important facts and he or she will make sure you are allowed to give any testimony significant in your case.

- Don't argue with the judge or the lawyers.
- Take your time. You may be asked some questions that call for a thoughtful response. If you need a moment to reflect on an answer before you give it, allow yourself that time.
- Stop speaking if an objection is made by one of the lawyers. Wait until the judge has decided whether to allow you to answer.
- If you begin to feel emotional, your lawyer can ask for a short break.

15.26 Should I be worried about being cross-examined by my spouse's lawyer at trial?

If your case goes to trial, prepare to be asked some questions by your spouse's lawyer. Many of these questions will call for a simple "yes" or "no."

If you are worried about particular questions, discuss your concerns with your attorney. He or she can support you in giving a truthful response. Focus on preparing well for being asked questions by your spouse's lawyer. Try not to take the questions personally; remember that the lawyer is fulfilling a duty to advocate for your spouse's interest. Remember that you are just doing your best to tell the truth about the facts.

15.27 What happens on the day of trial?

Although no two trials are alike, the following steps will occur in most divorce trials:

- Attorneys meet with the judge in chambers to discuss procedural issues, such as how many witnesses will be called, how long the case will take to present, and when breaks might be taken.
- Attorneys give opening statements.
- Petitioner's attorney calls petitioner's witnesses to testify.
- Respondent's attorney may cross-examine each of them.

212

- Respondent's attorney calls respondent's witness to testify. Petitioner's attorney may cross-examine each of them.

- Closing arguments are made first by the petitioner's attorney and then by the respondent's attorney.

15.28 Will the judge decide my case the day I go to court?

Probably not. Often there is so much information from the trial for the judge to consider that it is not possible for the judge to give an immediate ruling.

The judge may want to review documents, review the law, perform calculations, review his or her notes, and give thoughtful consideration to the issues to be decided. For this reason, it may be days, weeks, or in some cases, even longer before a ruling is made.

When a judge does not make a ruling immediately upon the conclusion of a trial, it is said that the case has been "taken under advisement."

16

The Appeals Process

You may find that despite your best efforts to settle your case, your divorce went to trial and the judge made major decisions that will have a serious impact on your future. You may be either gravely disappointed or even shocked by the judge's ruling.

The judge might have seen your case differently than you and your attorney did. Perhaps the judge made mistakes. Or it may be that Arizona law simply does not allow for the outcome you were hoping for.

Whatever the reasons for the court's rulings, you may feel that the judge's decisions are not ones that you can live with. If this is the case, talk to your lawyer immediately about your right to appeal. Together you can decide whether an appeal is in your best interest or whether it is better to accept the court's ruling and invest your energy in moving forward with your future without an appeal.

16.1 How much time after my divorce do I have to file an appeal?

You must file an appeal within thirty days of the final order you wish to appeal. Because your attorney may also recommend filing certain motions following your trial, such as a motion for new trial or a motion to amend the findings, discuss your appeal rights with your lawyer as soon as you have received the judge's ruling.

A timely discussion with your attorney about your right to appeal is essential so important deadlines are not missed.

16.2   Can I appeal a temporary order?

No. Under Arizona law, only final orders may be appealed.

16.3   What parts of the decree can be appealed?

If you or your spouse is unhappy with final decisions made by the judge in your case, either of you can file an appeal. Some of the decisions that can be appealed include legal decision-making, parenting time, child support, spousal maintenance, division of property, classification of the assets as sole and separate or community, the value of community assets, and attorney's fees.

16.4   Will my attorney recommend I appeal specific aspects of the decree, or will I have to request it?

Your attorney may counsel you to file an appeal on certain issues of your case; you may also ask your lawyer whether there is a legitimate basis for an appeal of any decision you believe is wrong. Talk to your attorney regarding the decisions most dissatisfying to you. Your lawyer can advise which issues have the greatest likelihood of success on appeal, in light of the facts of your case and Arizona law.

16.5   When should an appeal be filed?

An appeal should be filed only after careful consultation with your lawyer when you believe that the judge has made a serious error under the law or the facts of your case. Among the factors you and your attorney should discuss are:

- Whether the judge had the authority under the law to make the decisions set forth in your decree
- The likelihood of the success of your appeal
- The risk that an appeal by you will encourage an appeal by your former spouse
- The cost of the appeal
- The length of time an appeal can be expected to take
- The impact of a delay in the case during the appeal

The deadline for filing an appeal is thirty days from the date that a final order is entered in your case. It is important that you are clear about the deadline that applies in your case, so talk to your attorney at once if you are thinking about an appeal.

Before filing an a appeal, sometimes your lawyer may recommend filing a motion for new trial or motion to amend the findings. These motions are made to the trial judge and give the trial judge an opportunity to correct any mistakes made at trial. These motions are less expensive than an appeal, but must be done within fifteen days after the final order. Accordingly, do not delay in discussing with your lawyer any issues you are dissatisfied with and see whether a motion can be filed to correct the rulings.

16.6   Are there any disadvantages to filing an appeal?

There can be disadvantages to filing an appeal, including:

- Uncertainty as to the outcome
- Increased attorney's fees and costs
- The risks of a worse outcome on appeal than you received at trial
- Delay
- Prolonged conflict between you and your former spouse
- Risk of a second trial occurring after the appeal
- Difficulty in obtaining closure and moving forward with your life

16.7   Is an attorney necessary to appeal?

The appeals process is very detailed and specific, with set deadlines and specific court rules. Given the complex nature of the appellate process, you should have an attorney if you intend to file an appeal.

16.8   How long does the appeals process usually take?

It depends. An appeal can take anywhere from several months to well over a year. An appeal may also result in the appellate court requiring further proceedings by the trial court. This will result in further delay.

16.9   What are the steps in the appeals process?

There are many steps that your lawyer will take on your behalf in the appeal process, including:

- Identifying the issues to be appealed
- Filing a notice with the court of your intent to appeal
- Obtaining the necessary court documents and trial exhibits to send to the appellate court
- Obtaining a transcript of the trial, which is a written copy of testimony by witnesses and statements by the judge and the lawyers made in the presence of the court reporter
- Performing legal research to support your arguments on appeal
- Preparing and filing a document known as a *brief,* which sets forth the facts of the case and relevant law, complete with citations to court transcripts, court documents, and prior cases
- Making an oral argument before the judges of the appellate court

16.10 Is filing and pursuing an appeal expensive?

Yes. In addition to filing fees and lawyer fees, there is likely to be a substantial cost for the preparation of the transcript of the trial testimony.

16.11 If I do not file an appeal, can I ever go back to court to change my decree?

Certain aspects of a decree are not modifiable, such as the division of property and debts or the award of attorney fees. Other parts of your decree, such as support or matters regarding the children, may be modified if there has been a "changed circumstances that are substantial and continuing."

A modification of legal decision-making or parenting time for minor children will also require you to show that the change would be in their best interest.

If your decree did not provide for spousal maintenance or if it ordered that the spousal maintenance be nonmodifiable, it is unlikely that you will have any basis for a modification. If you believe that you have a basis for a modification of your divorce decree, consult with your attorney.

17

Postdivorce Considerations

Now that it is over, what happens next? You have concentrated so much on getting a divorce and now that it happened to you may be feeling confused, alone, and wondering what happens now.

Those feelings are not unusual. Your attorney has been walking this journey with you the entire time, and now you may feel as if you have no one to offer support and comfort to you.

Although it is true that the conclusion of your divorce may end the matter for which your attorney was retained, there are still a number of matters that need to be undertaken. The guidance of your attorney may still be necessary to ensure you are implementing the terms of your divorce decree correctly.

This chapter provides some guidance and a checklist for items that may need to be accomplished now that your divorce is final.

17.1   What do I need to do now that the divorce is over?

There are a number of items that need to be taken care of once the decree is entered and your case is final. Your lawyer will likely provide you with a closing letter that will detail some of the items in your decree that you must follow.

In addition, read your decree closely to determine what needs to be done to implement the terms. The following is a general checklist of some of the items that may need to be addressed (it is by no means inclusive of every possible issue):

- Obtain or transfer automobile and homeowner's insurance in your name.
- Make sure your health insurance is in place. Remember, if you are a dependent on your spouse's insurance, the insurance will terminate upon divorce.
- Life insurance beneficiaries are changed or in place if needed. Determine whether the ownership of life insurance needs to be changed.
- Determine how best to invest your financial assets to ensure your long-term goals are met.
- Refinance the mortgage on the marital residence if required by your decree.
- Make sure all qualified domestic relations orders (QDRO) are prepared and filed, that divide any related retirement plans.
- If you have changed addresses, give your new address to the court and post office.
- Work with an accountant or other professional to determine the tax ramifications of division of assets before any assets are sold or investments are liquidated. Determine whether you need to pay estimated quarterly taxes to the IRS or the state.
- If you have not already done so, close all joint financial accounts and credit cards.
- Change beneficiaries on financial accounts, retirement accounts, and life insurance if permitted by your decree.
- Amend your estate plan.
- If you have a judgment where your spouse owes you money, it must be renewed every five years.

17.2 I am moving out of the marital residence. How can I update my address with the court?

The court requires that you update your address and name with the court if there are any changes. This is especially important if you are receiving spousal maintenance or child support. A sample form that is used in Maricopa County is included in the Appendix. You may modify this form if your county does not have a form.

In some cases, local rules and forms may vary between counties. Be sure any form you modify complies with the local rules for the county in which you are filing. You may check with the clerk of the court or the self-service center in your county to makes sure the modified form complies with the local rules.

17.3 Our health plan states we need a *qualified medical support order*. What is that?

A *qualified medical support order (QMSO)* is a court order that requires certain health plans to provide coverage to children of divorce and separation. It is generally not necessary to obtain a separate order. Rather, if your decree provides for medical support of a child, it is considered a medical child support order for purposes of continuing coverage for the children.

17.4 The children are on my former spouse's health insurance. How can I obtain reimbursement for medical expenses I pay for the children?

Make sure that you are in possession of insurance cards for the minor children. If at all possible, have the health service provider bill the insurance directly so that you are not incurring expenses.

In cases where there are co-pays or services not covered by the provider, you may need to advance the funds. Determine if you can set up payment directly to you for reimbursement for out-of-pocket medical expenses versus having the reimbursements submitted to your former spouse.

You should also ascertain if you can receive a duplicate *explanation of benefits* form so that you can track medical reimbursements. Most plans will permit you access to the health benefits website to track benefits and information for the minor child in your custody.

If you encounter any problems, you may need to work directly with the human resources department of your former spouse's employer. The important thing to keep in mind is to ensure all steps are taken so that you have access to information on medical coverage for the minor children before services need to be performed.

17.5   My decree provides that my former spouse and I are to each pay a portion of unreimbursed medical expenses for the minor children. How do I track those expenses?

Be sure to provide your former spouse with appropriate documentation as set forth in your decree. Failure to request reimbursement for these expenses in a timely manner may bar you from being able to collect them.

Reimbursement for uninsured medical expenses as well as extracurricular activities and child-care expenses is an issue frequently disputed in post-decree modification and enforcement hearings. For this reason, maintain complete records regarding these expenses, such as:

- Keeping copies of billing statements from the service providers with your notations regarding payments made to include the date, amount, and check number
- Keeping copies of all insurance benefit statements
- Asking your pharmacy to give you a monthly or an annual printout of all the charges and payments for prescription drugs
- Asking your child-care provider to give you monthly or an annual printout of all charges and payments.
- Keeping copies of the statements and payments made for all extracurricular activities
- Keeping copies of all correspondence between you and the other parent regarding these expenses
- Keeping a record of the sums paid by the other parent, directly to providers, and all reimbursements made to you

Keep these records in a file folder labeled by child and year so that you have easy access. In the event of a future dispute, you will have all the information needed for your attorney to present your case or defend a claim against you.

A sample Unreimbursed Medical Expense Chart is included in the Appendix to help keep track of expenses. Use this form or modify one to fit your needs. Requests for reimbursements must be submitted within 180 days after the date of service occurs (or as provided in your decree) or you will be considered to have waived your claim.

17.6 My divorce decree provides for my name change. Is there anything else I need to do?

As part of your divorce decree, you will have the opportunity to restore your former name. Use the following as a checklist of people and places to notify of your name change:

- Banks and other financial institutions
- Financial planner, accountant
- Creditors (including mortgage company, auto loan companies, credit cards)
- Credit reporting agencies
- Motor Vehicle Department (for car registration and license)
- Employers
- Doctors, medical providers
- Post Office
- Passport office
- Social Security Administration
- Internal Revenue Service, Arizona Department of Revenue
- Utility companies
- Church/religious organizations
- Professional and alumni organizations
- Magazine/newspaper/publication subscriptions
- Stock certificates, deeds, and property titles
- Update address with the court and the Arizona Support Clearinghouse

Obtain several certified copies of your divorce decree if your name has been changed. You will need to provide or show a certified copy to the various agencies above.

In Closing

Now pause and take a deep breath. Acknowledge yourself for the courage you have shown in examining your unique situation, needs, and goals. Now, you are facing your future—recasting yourself into a new life. You are looking more closely at your living situation, the needs of your children, your financial security and your personal growth and healing. You are seeing your situation and telling the truth about what you now need. You are taking action to propel you into new possibilities.

From here, it is time to take inventory of the lessons learned, goals met, and action yet to take. Celebrate each of those steps forward and be gentle with yourself over the occasional misstep backward. You have transitioned through this time when everything is reduced to the core of you. Gone are the familiar habits of your marriage. With every day moving closer to the completion of your divorce, your grief will begin to subside and your energy improve as you move toward a fresh start. All the best to you as you accomplish this life journey.

Appendix

Chapter 2

A Child's Perspective on Divorce
If They Felt Like They Could Really Tell You
What They Are Really Thinking

1. I am not getting a divorce, you are. You are divorcing each other, but I am not divorcing either one of you. You are still both my parents, and that will not change after the divorce.
2. Please do not say negative things to me about the other parent. I love you both and it hurts me to hear you say bad things about the other parent. When you say negative things it just makes me mad at you for trying to make me feel bad about the other parent.
3. Please do not put me in the middle of your dispute. I am not going to take sides, and even if I did it would only be to satisfy you and make you stop talking about it.
4. Please do not use me to communicate messages to the other parent. If you have something to say to the other parent, please find a way to communicate to them directly. I am likely to get the message wrong anyway.
5. Do not ask me about what the other parent is doing, who they are seeing, or try to get "information" from me about the other parent. That makes me feel like a traitor if I give you information, or it makes me

feel like you want me to spy on the other parent. I don't want to be put in this position. Besides, I don't know everything anyway and you are likely to get a misimpression of the circumstances.

6. Please do not get into fights with the other parent over their parenting skills. If the other parent is not exercising the same parenting skills that you would it does not mean they are a bad parent. It just means they parent differently than you. If you fight about this, I will learn that I can play one parent off the other. I know that rules are different in each house and I can learn to respect each parent's rules.

7. I understand you may not want me to see my friends or have a sleepover at a friend's house because you feel like you are losing parent time. That's okay. I will learn to adjust, but I hope you will let me speak up and talk to you about it. Please be open and honest about your feelings with me, rather than just saying no, and I will be open and honest with you about my feelings. Hopefully, we can compromise.

8. Please do not use money that you may be receiving or giving to the other parent as a way to punish me. Saying things like, you don't receive enough money, or you already give money for a particular activity, puts me in the middle. Please try to work out these issues with the other parent without me, and then jointly tell me your decision. I can understand "no" coming from both of you. This is part of what co-parenting should be about. A simple "I will discuss it with your mother/father" is all I need to hear.

9. I know that someday you may have another person in your life. I am okay with that. Just take it slow and introduce me gradually to the other person. Do not expect us to become an instant family.

10. Please do not argue over holidays with the other parent. I can be flexible. Please be flexible too. It is only a date on a calendar. If you make it a positive choice, rather than a negative, we can celebrate two Thanksgivings, two Christmases, two of everything,

and I will consider myself the luckiest kid in the world for getting to do everything twice with the two people I love the most.

Chapter 3

Choosing a Lawyer

If you decide to retain a lawyer, take your time in choosing the lawyer who is right for your particular case. Set up a consultation with the lawyer in advance to retaining him or her so you have an opportunity to ask questions and determine whether their style fits your needs. This is a journey that you will be taking together with your attorney as they help you reach the end result. Retaining someone who not only is competent in family law, but who you feel comfortable talking with, is paramount.

You will be sharing very personal details of your married life, your goals for the future, and expected outcomes. You need to feel a connection with the person who you are entrusting to help you with decisions concerning your financial future, as well as, if you have children, decisions about parenting time Make sure the person is someone you feel understands your situation and concerns.

You should feel free to interview at least two or three attorneys so you have an understanding of the different styles of each attorney. Although you may be paying for multiple consultations, finding an attorney who is the right fit will save you countless hours of frustration later. You will know when the person you meet with is right for you.

The following is a list of questions you may want to ask during the first consultation to help you obtain a better understanding about the lawyer's expertise as well as whether the attorney's work style and your style are similar enough to make for a good working relationship.

1. What is your particular experience in family law and in handling this type of situation in particular? Are you a certified specialist by the State Bar of Arizona? Do you handle matters other than family law?

2. Do you work evenings and weekends? If something occurs of importance over the weekend, what is your policy for addressing those issues?

3. Will you personally be handling my case or will other lawyers or paralegals be assisting?
4. What is the best way to communicate with you? (Telephone? E-mail?) How do you charge for each?
5. Do you have a policy on how long before you return a telephone call?
6. How many times do you expect that we will need to meet in person? Under what circumstances will we need to meet in person?
7. What are the specific steps in the divorce process and how long do you expect it to take?
8. What is the likely cost? (This will be a difficult question for your lawyer to answer. Be wary if you are given a specific cost since so many variables exist that are unknown at the initial consultation. The lawyer may, however, be able to give you an idea of what similar cases have cost or the potential range of costs depending on whether the action is contested, settled, or litigated.)
9. Will there be a need to hire other individuals to assist with the divorce such as financial planners, valuation experts, forensic accountants, or vocational evaluators? If so, what are the likely expenses for these individuals?
10. If I do not have access to all the financial information, how will the information be obtained?
11. Based upon the situation that I have explained, what do you see as the most challenging aspects of my case? How do you believe these challenges should be handled? What is the likely outcome?
12. Is this a case that may be resolved in mediation or some other dispute resolution process? Why or why not?
13. Are there any steps that I should take now to protect myself financially?
14. What are the first steps you would take if I were to retain you?

The lawyer you are considering may not have answers to every question, and rarely can they predict so early in the case what the likely outcome will be. The point of asking the questions, though, is not necessarily to obtain precise answers, but to find out if the lawyer you are consulting with is someone you feel will be able to represent your best interests in a way that is satisfactory to you.

Chapter 5
Categories of Deposition Questions

Regardless of the specific issues in your case, there are general categories that virtually all depositions in a dissolution of marriage action will cover. Your attorney will go over specific questions and categories with you. However, a general outline of the categories that you should be prepared to testify about is as follows:

1. *Background Questions.* Date of marriage, last time lived together, where living now, children (ages and school)

2. *Employment.* Where you are currently working, where you worked previously, when you were last employed, why you quit, what efforts have been made to locate employment (if not working)

3. *Health and Mental State.* Current health condition and mental state, whether you are under any doctor's care, or taking any prescribed medications, whether you are seeing a counselor, and if so the purpose, frequency and name of counselor

4. *Property Division.* What assets exist, whether you consider any of these assets your sole and separate property, and if so which ones and how were they acquired, how you would like to see property divided, what income can you expect to earn off of the liquid assets, what vehicles exist including make, mileage, condition

5. *Expenses.* What expenses you have, how they are being paid, whether they are the normal and reasonable expenses incurred during the marriage, how the

numbers on your affidavit of financial information were determined

6. *Appraisals.* Whether you have had any appraisals done to determine the value of any of the marital property (house, cars, community businesses)

7. *Property. a.)* Vehicles. Make, year, registration, Insurance, condition, inspection, repair records. Although a deposition may be rather intimidating at first, this is a wonderful opportunity to prepare for trial and will make you that much better in giving trial testimony. Just remember, take your time, speak slowly and tell the truth, and your deposition will go very smoothly. *b.)* House. Who holds title, when purchased, funds used for purchase. *c.)* Financial accounts. How many, where held, what funds were withdrawn. *d.)* Retirement accounts. Type of accounts, who holds, where held at, approximate balances. *e.)* Investment accounts. Stocks, bonds, options.

8. *Businesses.* Community businesses, sole and separate businesses, when started, how operated

9. *Children.* Questions regarding decision-making, visitation, holidays, school expenses, extracurricular activities, qualities of the other parent that are beneficial to the children, qualities that are harmful to the children.

Chapter 8
Holiday Parenting Plan

Parties can pick and choose the holidays and school breaks that they would like to include.

Winter Break: Commences when school is released until school resumes. Mother shall have the first week of the break in all even years. Father shall have the second week of the break in all odd years thereafter. Christmas Eve and Christmas Day take precedent over Winter Break.

Christmas Eve is defined as 5:00 P.M. on December 24 and ends at 10:00 A.M. on December 25. Mother shall have Christmas Eve in odd years. Father shall have Christmas Eve in even years.

Appendix

Christmas Day is defined as 10:00 A.M. on December 25 to 10:00 A.M. on December 26. Mother shall have Christmas Day in even years. Father shall have Christmas Day in odd years.

Passover is defined as 3:00 P.M. on the first night of Passover until drop-off at school the following morning (or 9:00 A.M. if no school). Mother shall have Passover in even years. Father shall have Passover in odd years.

Rosh Hashanah is defined as 3:00 P.M. the night before until the day following Rosh Hashanah drop-off at school (or 9:00 A.M. if no school). Mother shall have Rosh Hashanah in odd years. Father shall have Rosh Hashanah in even years.

Yom Kippur is defined as 3:00 P.M. the night before until the day following Yom Kippur drop-off at school (or 9:00 A.M. if no school). Mother shall have Yom Kippur in even years. Father shall have Yom Kippur in odd years.

Thanksgiving is defined as from Wednesday after school until Monday back to school. Father shall have Thanksgiving in even years. Mother shall have Thanksgiving in odd years.

Fall/Spring Break: Commences Sunday night before the break to Sunday before the return to school. Mother shall have all even years. Father shall have all odd years.

Easter Day is defined as 9:00 A.M. on Easter Day until 7:00 P.M. on Easter Day. Mother shall have Easter in all odd years. Father shall have Easter in all even years.

Mother's Day is defined as from Saturday at 8:00 P.M. until Sunday at 8:00 P.M. Celebrated with Mother every year.

Father's Day is defined as from Saturday at 8:00 P.M. until Sunday at 8:00 P.M. Celebrated with Father every year.

4th of July: Follow regular schedule.

Halloween: Follow regular schedule.

Child's Birthdays: Follow regular schedule and celebrate when parent has parenting time.

Parents' Birthdays: Follow regular schedule and celebrate when parent has parenting time.

Monday holidays: Follow regular schedule.

Chapter 10
Affidavit of Financial Information

Name:_____
Mailing Address:_____
City, State, Zip Code:_____
Daytime Phone Number:_____
Evening Phone Number:_____
Representing: ☐Self ☐Petitioner ☐Respondent
State Bar Number:_____

For Clerk's Use Only

SUPERIOR COURT OF ARIZONA IN MARICOPA COUNTY

_____

Case No._____

ATLAS NO._____

Petitioner/Plaintiff

AFFIDAVIT OF FINANCIAL INFORMATION

_____

Respondent

Affidavit of_____

(Name of Person Whose Information is on this Affidavit)

Important Information About This Document

WARNING TO BOTH PARTIES: This Affidavit is an important document. You must fill out this Affidavit completely, and provide accurate information. You must provide copies of this Affidavit and all other required documents to the other party and to the judge. If you do not do this, the court may order you to pay a fine.

I have read the following document and know of my own knowledge that the facts and financial information stated below are true and correct, and that any false information may constitute perjury by me. I also understand that, if I fail to provide the required information or give misinformation, the judge may order sanctions against me, including assessment of fees for fines under Rule 31, Arizona Rules of Family Law Procedure.

_____

Date

Signature of the Person Making Affidavit

INSTRUCTIONS:

1. **Complete the entire Affidavit in black ink. If the spaces provided on this form are inadequate, use separate sheets of paper to complete the answers and attach them to the Affidavit. Answer every question completely! You must complete every blank. If you do not know the answer to a question or are guessing, please state that. If a question does not apply, write "NA" for "not applicable" to indicate your read the question. Round all amounts of money to the nearest dollar.**

2. Answer the following statements **YES** or **NO**. If you mark **NO**, explain your answer on a separate piece of paper and attach the explanation to the Affidavit.

   ☐Yes   ☐No   I listed all sources of my income.

   ☐Yes   ☐No   I attached copies of my two (2) most recent pay stubs.

   ☐Yes   ☐No   I attached copies of my federal income tax return for the last three (3) years, and I attached my W-2 and 1099 forms from all sources of income.

1. GENERAL INFORMATION:

A. Name:_____ Date of Birth:_____

B. Current Address:_____

C. Date of Marriage:_____ Date of Divorce:_____

D. Last date when you and the other party lived together:_____

E. Full names of child(ren) common to the parties (in this case), their dates of birth:

Name   Date of Birth

_____   _____

_____   _____

_____   _____

Appendix

Case No._____

F. The name, date of birth, relationship to you, and gross monthly income for each individual who lives in your household:

Name	Date of Birth	Relationship to you	Income
_____	_____	_____	_____
_____	_____	_____	_____

G. Any other person for whom you contribute support:

Name	Age	Relationship to you	Reside with you (Y/N)	Court Order to support (Y/N)
_____	___	_____	_____	_____
_____	___	_____	_____	_____

H. Attorney's Fees paid in the matter $_____Source of funds_____

2. EMPLOYMENT INFORMATION:

A. Your job/occupation/profession/title:_____

   Name and address of current employer:_____

   _____

   Date employment began:_____

   How often are you paid: ☐ Weekly ☐ Every other week ☐ Twice a month

   ☐ Other_____

B. If you are not working, why not?_____

C. Previous employer name and address:_____

   _____

   Previous job/occupation/profession/title:_____

   Date previous job began:_____Date previous job ended:_____

   Reason you left job:_____

   Gross monthly pay at previous job:$_____

D. Total gross income from the last three (3) years' tax returns (attach copies of pages 1 and 2 of your federal income tax returns for the last three (3) years):

   Year_____$_____Year_____$_____Year_____$_____

E. Your total gross income from January 1 of this year to the date of the this Affidavit (year to date income)

   $_____

3. YOUR EDUCATION/TRAINING: List name of school, length of time there, year of last attendance, and degree earned:

A. High School:_____

B. College:_____

C. Post-Graduate:_____

D. Occupational Training:_____

4. YOUR GROSS MONTHLY INCOME:

- List **all** income you receive from **any** source, whether private or governmental, taxable or not.
- List all income payable to you individually or payable jointly to you or your spouse.
- Use a monthly average for items that vary from month to month.
- Multiply weekly income and deductions by 4.33. Multiply biweekly income by 2.165 to arrive at the total amount for the month.

A. Gross salary/wages per month $_____

- **Attach copies of your two most recent pay stubs.**

   Rate of Pay$_____per ☐ hour ☐ week ☐ month ☐ year

B. Expenses paid by your employer:

   1.   Automobile $_____

   2.   Auto expenses, such as gas, repairs, insurance $_____

233

Case No._____
  1.   Lodging $_____
  2.   Other (Explain) $_____
  C. Commissions/Bonuses $_____
  D. Tips $_____
  E. Self-employment Income (See below) $_____
  F. Social Security benefits $_____
  G. Worker's compensation and/or disability income $_____
  H. Unemployment compensation $_____
  I. Gifts/Prizes $_____
  J. Payments from prior spouse $_____
  K. Rental income (net after expenses) $_____
  L. Contributions to household living expenses by others $_____
  M. Other (Explain:)_____
     Include dividends, pensions, interest, trust income, annuities, or royalties.)
                                                    TOTAL: $_____

5. SELF-EMPLOYMENT INCOME (if applicable):

If you are self-employed, attach a copy of the Schedule C for your business from your last tax return and the most recent income/expense statement from your business.
If self-employed, provide the following information:
Name, address, and telephone number of the business_____
_____
Type of business entity:_____
State and Date of incorporation:_____
Nature of your business:_____
Percent of ownership:_____
Number of shares of stock:_____
Total issued and outstanding shares:_____
Gross sales/revenue last 12 months:_____

INSTRUCTIONS
Both parties must answer item 6 if either party asks for child support. These expenses include only those expenses for children who are common to the parties, which means one party is the birth/adoptive mother and the other is the birth/adoptive father of the children.

---

6. SCHEDULE OF ALL MONTHLY EXPENSES FOR CHILDREN:
  • **DO NOT LIST** any expenses for the other party, or child(ren) who live(s) with the other party, **unless** you are paying those expenses.
  • Use a monthly average for items that vary from month to month.
  • If you are listing anticipated expenses, indicate this by putting an asterisk (*) next to the estimated amount.

A. HEALTH INSURANCE:
  Do you have health insurance? ☐ Yes ☐ No   **Are you enrolled?**_____
  1. Total monthly cost $_____
  2. Premium cost to insure you alone $_____
  3. Premium cost to insure child(ren) common to the parties $_____
  4. List all people covered by your insurance coverage.
  _____
  _____
  5.   Name of insurance company and Policy/Group Number:
  _____

Appendix

Case No._____

B. HEALTH INSURANCE:
    Do you have health insurance? ☐ Yes ☐ No   **Are you enrolled?**_____
    1. Total monthly cost $_____
    2. Premium cost to insure you alone $_____
    3. Premium cost to insure child(ren) common to the parties $_____
    4. List all people covered by your insurance coverage.
    _____
    _____
    5. Name of insurance company and Policy/Group Number:
    _____

C. UNREIMBURSED MEDICAL AND DENTAL EXPENSES:
    (Cost to you after, or in addition to, any insurance reimbursement)
    1. Drugs and medical supplies $_____
    2. Other $_____
        TOTAL: $_____

D. CHILD CARE COSTS:
    1. Total monthly child care costs $_____
        (Do not include amounts paid by D.E.S.)
    2. Name(s) of child(ren) cared for and amount per child:
    _____ $_____
    _____ $_____
    _____ $_____
    3. Name(s) and address(es) of child care provider(s):
    _____
    _____

E. EMPLOYER PRETAX PROGRAM:
    Do you participate in an employer program for pretax payment of child care expenses?
    (Cafeteria Plan)? ☐ **Yes** ☐ **No**

F. COURT ORDERED CHILD SUPPORT:
    1. Court ordered current child support for child(ren)
        not common to the parties $_____
    2. Court ordered cash medical support for child(ren)
        not common to the parties $_____
    3. Amount of any arrears payment $_____
    4. Amount per month actually paid in last 12 months $_____
        • Attach proof that you are paying
    5. Name(s) and relationship of minor child(ren) who you support or who live with you, but are **not**
        common to the parties.
    _____
    _____

G. COURT ORDERED SPOUSAL MAINTENANCE/SUPPORT (Alimony):
    1. Court ordered spousal maintenance/support you actually
        pay to previous spouse. $_____

Case No._____

H. EXTRAORDINARY EXPENSES:

1. For **Children** (Educational Expense/Special Needs/Other): $_____
   Explain:_____

   _____

2. For **Self:** $_____
   Explain:_____

   _____

INSTRUCTIONS

Both parties must answer items 7 and 8 if either party is requesting:
- Spousal maintenance
- Division of expenses
- Attorneys' fees and costs
- Adjustment of deviation from the child support amount
- Enforcement

---

7. SCHEDULE OF ALL MONTHLY EXPENSES:

- **DO NOT LIST** any expenses for the other party, or child(ren) who live(s) with the other party, **unless** you are paying those expenses
- Use a monthly average for items that vary from month to month.
- If you are listing anticipated expenses, indicate this by putting an asterisk (*) next to the estimated amount.

A. HOUSING EXPENSES:

1. House payment:
   a. First Mortgage $_____
   b. Second Mortgage $_____
   c. Homeowners Association Fee $_____
   d. Rent $_____
2. Repair and upkeep $_____
3. Yard work/Pool/Pest Control $_____
4. Insurance and taxes not included in house payment $_____
5. Other (Explain:)_____ $_____
   TOTAL $_____

B. UTILITIES:

1. Water, sewer, and garbage $_____
2. Electricity $_____
3. Gas $_____
4. Telephone $_____
5. Mobile phone/pager $_____
6. Internet Provider $_____
7. Cable/Satellite television $_____
8. Other (Explain:)_____ $_____
   TOTAL $_____

C. FOOD:

1. Food, milk, and household supplies $_____
2. School lunches $_____
3. Meals outside the home $_____
   TOTAL $_____

236

Case No._____

D. CLOTHING:
   1. Clothing for you $_____
   2. Uniforms or special work clothes $_____
   3. Clothing for children living with you $_____
   4. Laundry and cleaning $_____
                         TOTAL $_____

E. TRANSPORTATION OR AUTOMOBILE EXPENSES:
   1. Car insurance $_____
   2. List all cars and individuals covered:

     _____

     _____

   3. Car payment, if any $_____
   4. Car repair and maintenance $_____
   5. Gas and oil $_____
   6. Bus fare/parking fees $_____
   7. Other (Explain:)_____ $_____
                         TOTAL $_____

F. MISCELLANEOUS:
   1. School and school supplies $_____
   2. School activities or fees $_____
   3. Extracurricular activities of child(ren) $_____
   4. Church/contributions $_____
   5. Newspapers, magazines, and books $_____
   6. Barber and beauty shop $_____
   7. Life insurance (beneficiary:_____) $_____
   8. Disability insurance $_____
   9. Recreation/entertainment $_____
  10. Child(ren)'s allowance(s) $_____
  11. Union/Professional dues $_____
  12. Voluntary retirement contributions $_____
  13. Family gifts $_____
  14. Pet expenses $_____
  15. Cigarettes $_____
  16. Alcohol $_____
  17. Other (Explain:)_____ $_____
                       TOTAL $_____

Case No._____

8. OUTSTANDING DEBTS AND ACCOUNTS: List all debts and installment payments you currently owe, but do not include items listed in Item 7 "Monthly Schedule of Expenses." Follow the format below. Use additional paper if necessary.

Creditor Name	Purpose of Debt	Unpaid Balance	Min. Monthly Payment	Date of Your Last Payment	Amount of Your Payment

Chapter 11
Inventory of Property and Debts

Name:_____
Mailing Address:_____
City, State, Zip Code:_____
Daytime Phone Number:_____
Evening Phone Number:_____
Representing: ☐Self ☐Petitioner ☐Respondent
State Bar Number:_____

SUPERIOR COURT OF ARIZONA IN _____ COUNTY

_____   Case No._____

Petitioner

_____   ATLAS NO._____
                                         INVENTORY OF PROPERTY AND DEBTS
Respondent   ☐Husband
                                         ☐Wife

I. PROPERTY

List all property acquired during your marriage in which you or your spouse claims to have a community interest. If there is a dispute as to whether there is a community interest or obligation, indicate under "Contested Position." Value of the property is its current fair market value, minus any encumbrances. Use additional paper if necessary.

Description	Date Acquired	Value	Contested Position	Proposed Allocation [H or W]

A. Cash and Financial Institution Accounts: savings, checking, money market, etc. Include financial institution's name, branch, and account number.

B. Investments: stocks, bonds, notes, certificates of deposit, mortgages, deeds of trust, etc.

Description	Date Acquired	Value	Contested Position	Proposed allocation [H or W]

C. Life Insurance: company name, owner, policy number, insured, beneficiary, death benefits and cash surrender value (if any)

D. Retirement Plans: pension, profit-sharing, 401(k), deferred compensation

E. Real Property:

F. Business Interests: corporations, partnerships, limited liability corporations, joint ventures, proprietorships

G. Vehicles: cars, motorcycles, motor homes, boats, trailers, etc.

Appendix

Description	Date Acquired	Value	Contested Position	Proposed allocation [H or W]

H. Personal Property over $100 in Value: household goods, personal effects, antiques, objects of intrinsic value

Description	Date Acquired	Value	Contested Position	Proposed allocation [H or W]

I. Miscellaneous Assets:

II. DEBTS

List all debts and installment payments you currently owe. Use additional paper if necessary.

Creditor Name	Purpose of Debt	Unpaid Balance	Min. Monthly Payment	Date of Last Payment	Contested Position	Proposed Allocation [H or W]

Appendix

Creditor Name	Purpose of Debt	Unpaid Balance	Min. Monthly Payment	Date of Last Payment	Contested Position	Proposed Allocation [H or W]

Date

Signature of
☐ Husband ☐ Wife
☐ Attorney for ☐ Husband ☐ Wife

Chapter 17
Name or Address Information Update

Name:_____

Address:_____

Telephone Number:_____

E-mail:_____

SUPERIOR COURT OF ARIZONA IN MARICOPA COUNTY

In re the Marriage of:

No._____

_____

Petitioner,

and

_____

Respondent,

UPDATE INFORMATION ON
☐ **ADDRESS and/ or**
☐ **NAME**

IF YOUR ADDRESS IS PROTECTED BY COURT ORDER DO <u>NOT USE THIS FORM</u>

I Understand:
1. This Notice is to tell the Clerk of the Court that my address or name has changed.
2. This form does NOT legally change my name.
3. Address and name changes that are not sealed or confidential will be entered on both the support payment and the court's automated system, and will be available to the public record.
4. I may only submit changes for *my own* address and name.

INFORMATION I WANT TO CHANGE: (PLEASE PRINT)

My name *was*:_____

My current name is:_____

My *old* address was:_____
(Street Address, City, State, Zip Code)
_____

My *new* address is:_____
(Street Address, City, State, Zip Code)
_____

My new *mailing* address:_____
(If different from above)
_____

My best contact phone number is: (___)_____**My Date of Birth is:**_____

My e-mail address is:_____

☐ There is an order for payments through the Clearinghouse for **Child Support and/or Spousal Maintenance** (if so, fax to **602-506-1937**). *OR*

☐ There is an order for payments through the Clerk of the Superior Court for Restitution (if so, e-mail the completed form to: CFOResponse@mail.maricopa.gov) *OR*

☐ This update is for *other than* Support, Maintenance, or Restitution (if so, fax to **602-506-6690**).

I declare under penalty of perjury that the foregoing is true and correct.

Signed on:_____   _____
Date   Signature of Person Requesting Change

☐ Please send me information on direct deposit for Child Support and/or Spousal Maintenance.

☐ **iCIS Address updated** (FOR COURT USE ONLY)

UNREIMBURSED MEDICAL, DENTAL AND VISION CARE EXPENSES

Case Number: _____

Father's Name: _____ Father's share of all unreimbursed expenses listed on this sheet is: _____

Mother's Name: _____ Mother's share of all unreimbursed expenses listed on this sheet is: _____

Total: 100%

Date of Service (oldest first)	Name of Health Care Provider	Total Amount of Bill	Amount of Bill Paid by Insurance or 3rd party	Amount of Bill Paid by Father	Amount of Bill Paid by Mother	Remaining Balance of Bill Due	Amount of Father's Remaining Responsibility	Amount of Mother's Remaining Responsibility
Total this sheet		$	$	$	$	$	$	

Resources

The following is a list of websites that may be of assistance to you.

State Bar of Arizona
www.azbar.org/workingwithlawyers/topics/understandingdivorce

Maricopa County Self Service Center
www.superiorcourt.maricopa.gov/ezcourtforms2/

Pima County Family Law Links
www.sc.pima.gov/?tabid=208

Certified Specialists in Family Law
www.azbar.org/workingwithlawyers/topics/certifiedlegalspecialist

Child Support Payment History
http://familysupportcenter.maricopa.gov/DES/default.asp

Information about Qualified Medical Support Orders
www.dol.gov/sites/default/files/ebsa/about-ebsa/our-activities/resource-center/publications/qualified-medical-child-support-orders.pdf

Arizona Support Payment Clearinghouse
PO Box 52107
Phoenix, Arizona 85072-2107
https://des.az.gov/

Helpful Telephone Numbers

Arizona's Child Support Enforcement Hotline
(602) 252-4045 or (800) 882-4151

Arizona Coalition Against Domestic Violence
Legal Advocacy Hotline: (800) 782-6400
Monday through Friday 8:30 P.M.—5:00 P.M.

Arizona Support Clearinghouse
(602) 252-4045

Community Legal Services
Kingman	(928) 681-1177 or (800) 255-9031
Mesa	(480) 833-1442 or (800) 896-3631
Phoenix	(602) 258-3434 or (800) 852-9075
Prescott	(928) 445-9240 or (800) 233-5114
San Luis	(928) 627-8023 or (800) 356-7115
Yuma	(928) 782-7511 or (800) 424-7962

DNA People's Legal Services, Inc.
Chinle	(928) 674-5242 or (800) 789-7598
Flagstaff	(928) 774-0653 or (800) 789-5781
Hopi	(928) 738-2251 or (800) 789-9586
Tuba City	(928) 283-5265 or (800) 789-8919
Window Rock	(928) 871-4151 or (800) 789-7287

Family Lawyers Assistance Project
(602) 506-7948

Maricopa County Family Support Center
(602) 506-3762

Southern Arizona Legal Aid, Inc.
Cochise/Graham/Greenlee County
(520) 432-1639 or (800) 231-7106

Four Rivers Indian Legal Services
(620) 562-3369 or (866) 312-2290

Gila/Navajo/Apache County
(928) 537-8388 or (800) 658-7958

Pima County
(520) 623-9465 or (800) 640-9465

Pinal County
(520) 316-8076 or (877) 718-8086

Tohono O'odham
(520) 623-9465 or (800) 640-9465

White Mountain Apache Services
(928) 338-4845 or (866) 312-2291

Maricopa County Bar Association
Lawyer Referral Service
(602) 257-4434

Pima County Bar Association
Lawyer Referral Service
(520) 623-4625

Glossary

affidavit: A written statement of facts made under oath and signed before a notary public. Affidavits are used primarily when there will not be a hearing in open court with live testimony. The attorney will prepare an affidavit to present relevant facts. Affidavits may be signed by the parties or in some cases by witnesses. The person signing the affidavit may be referred to as the *affiant*.

affidavit of financial information: The form provided to the court that details the income and expenses of the parties.

allegation: A statement that one party claims is true.

appeal: The process by which a higher court reviews the decision of a lower court. In Arizona family law cases, a person will first file an appeal with the Arizona Court of Appeals. After that appeal is decided there may be a further appeal to the Arizona Supreme Court.

best interest attorney: An attorney appointed by the court who has the duty to represent the best interest of the child.

child support: Financial support for a child paid by one parent to the other parent.

children's attorney: A children's attorney represents the child and advocates, just as any other attorney in the case, for his or her client's position.

collaborative divorce: An alternative dispute resolution that is designed to assist parties who have a strong commitment to amicably resolving their disputes and avoiding litigation.

conciliation services: A service available in some courts as a means to put the divorce action on hold until there is an opportunity to meet with a court representative and determine whether there is the ability to repair the marriage.

ccontempt of court: The willful and intentional failure of a party to comply with a court order, judgment, or decree. Contempt may be punishable by a fine or jail.

contested case: Any case in which the parties cannot reach an agreement. A contested case will result in a trial to have the judge decide disputed issues.

cross-examination: The questioning of a witness by the opposing counsel during trial or at a deposition, in response to questions asked by the other lawyer.

court appointed advisor: A person, often a lawyer or mental health professional, appointed by a court to conduct an investigation regarding the children's best interest and report to the court.

court order: A court-issued document setting forth the judge's orders. An order can be issued based upon the parties' agreement or the judge's decision. An order may require the parties to perform certain acts or set forth their rights and responsibilities. An order is put in writing, signed by the judge, and filed with the court.

decree of dissolution: A final court order dissolving the marriage, dividing property and debts, ordering support, and entering other orders regarding finances and the minor children.

deposition: A witness's testimony taken out of court, under oath, and in the presence of lawyers and a court reporter. If a person gives a different testimony at the time of trial, he or she can be impeached with the deposition testimony; that is, statements made at a deposition can be used to show untruthfulness if a different answer is given at trial.

direct examination: The initial questioning of a witness in court by the lawyer who called him or her to the stand.

discovery: A process used by attorneys to discover information from the opposing party for the purpose of fully assessing a case for settlement or trial. Types of discovery include interrogatories, requests for production of documents, and requests for admissions.

dissolution: The act of terminating or dissolving a marriage.

Glossary

ex parte: Usually in reference to a motion, the term used to describe an appearance of only one party before the judge, without the other party being present.

hearing: Any proceeding before the court for the purpose of resolving disputed issues between the parties through presentation of testimony, affidavits, exhibits, or argument.

hold-harmless clause: A term in a court order that requires one party to assume responsibility for a debt and to protect the other spouse from any loss or expense in connection with it, as in "to hold harmless from liability."

interrogatories: Written questions sent from one party to the other that are used to obtain facts or opinions related to the divorce.

joint legal decision-making: The shared right and responsibility of both parents awarded by the court for decision-making for children on education, health, and religion.

mediation: A process by which a neutral third party facilitates negotiations between the parties on a wide range of issues.

motion: A written application to the court for relief, such as temporary child support, temporary spousal maintenance, and parenting time.

motion to modify (sometimes called a *petition to modify*): A party's written request to the court to change a prior order regarding legal decision-making, parenting time, child support, spousal maintenance, or any other order that the court may change by law.

no-fault divorce: The type of divorce Arizona has that the court does not require evidence of marital misconduct. This means that abandonment, cruelty, and adultery are neither relevant nor required to be proven for the purposes of granting the divorce.

notice of hearing: A written statement sent to the opposing lawyer or spouse listing the date and place of a hearing and the nature of the matters that will be heard by the court. In Arizona, the party requesting the hearing is required to give the other party reasonable notice of any court hearing set by the court unless the court has given notice to both parties.

notice of intent to relocate: A parent's written notice to the other parent to relocate to another state with the minor children.

order to show cause: Written application to the court that requires the other person to appear and show cause why they should not be held in contempt of court for violating or failing to comply with a current court order.

parenting coordinator: An attorney or mental health professional who will attempt to help the parties resolve their issues with each other and, if not, make recommendations to the court on the day to day issues experienced by parents.

party: The person in a legal action whose rights or interest will be affected by the divorce. For example, in a divorce the parties include the wife and husband.

pending: During the case. For example, the judge may award you temporary support while your case is pending.

petition: The first document filed with the clerk of the court in an action for divorce, separation, or paternity. The petition sets forth the facts on which the requested relief is based.

petitioner: A term used to refer to the person filing the petition for dissolution, legal separation, or paternity. In civil actions this party is referred to by the more common name of *plaintiff.*

pleadings: Documents filed with the court seeking a court order.

preliminary injunction An order of the court prohibiting a party from certain behavior. For example, the preliminary injunction prohibits a party from selling community property or taking a minor child out of the state without permission.

qualified domestic relations order (QDRO): A type of court order that provides for direct payment from a retirement account to a former spouse.

request for production of documents: A written request for documents sent from one party to the other during the discovery process.

resolution management conference: A brief hearing held with the judge to advise the court of the nature of the matter and issues for trial.

respondent: The person responding to the dissolution, legal separation, or paternity action. In civil actions this party is referred to by the more common name of *defendant.*

Glossary

response to petition for dissolution or legal separation: A written response to the petition for divorce. It serves to admit or deny the allegations in the petition and may also make claims against the opposing party. The response should be filed within twenty days of either (a) the petitioner being served on the respondent or (b) the respondent voluntarily acknowledged service.

sealed case: A case that is not open to the public. The court may determine the interest of privacy of the individuals outweighs the rights of the public, and in order to protect the parties and the minor children may seal some or all portions of the case.

separate property: Any property acquired before the marriage, as well as property acquired during the marriage by gift, inheritance, or bequest. In addition, property acquired after service of the petition for dissolution of marriage or petition for legal separation is considered separate property if a decree of dissolution or legal separation is actually entered.

setoff: A debt or financial obligation of one spouse that is deducted from the debt or financial obligation of the other spouse.

settlement: The agreed resolution of disputed issues.

sole legal decision-making: The legal right and responsibility awarded by a court that gives one parent responsibility for making the decisions as to education, health, and religious matters for the minor children.

spousal maintenance: Court-ordered spousal support payments from one party to another, often to enable the recipient spouse to become economically independent.

stipulation: An agreement reached between parties or an agreement by their attorneys.

subpoena: A document delivered to a person or witness that requires him or her to appear in court, appear for a deposition, or produce documents. Failure to comply could result in punishment by the court. A subpoena requesting documents is called a *subpoena duces tecum.*

trial: A formal court hearing in which the judge will decide disputed issues raised by the parties' pleadings.

under advisement: A term used to describe the status of a case, usually after a court hearing on a motion or a trial, when the judge has not yet made a decision.

Index

Index

Index

Index

Index

Index

270

Index

superior court, 7, 28, 63, 96
supervised visitation, 99, 120, 121
support groups, 32
support orders, 18, 22
support payments, 20
support professionals, 62
survivor benefits, 181

T

tax advisors, 192, 194, 195, 197, 198, 199
tax consequences, 40, 172, 193, 196, 219
tax exemptions, 24, 198
tax filing status, 194
tax law, 198, 199
tax liabilities, 142
tax planning, 199
tax returns, 41, 62, 69, 88, 151
  correcting erroneous
  information, 151
taxes, 148, 152, 186, 192–199
  child support, 193
  documentation, 195
  spousal maintenance, 193, 194
telephonic court hearings, 201
Temporary Assistance to Needy Families program, 141
temporary child support, 131, 204
  steps in process, 132
temporary court orders, 18
temporary hearing, 6, 15, 27, 132, 207
temporary housing, 101
temporary order, 5, 24, 42, 49, 50, 57, 64, 74, 101, 106, 107, 110, 125, 186, 204
  appealing, 215
  hearing dates, 5
temporary orders hearing, 20, 21
  preparation for, 21

temporary parenting time, 204
temporary restraining orders (TRO), 97, 98
temporary spousal maintenance, 5, 204
tender years doctrine, 105
termination of child support, 22
testimony, 98
  at trial, 35
testimony of witnesses, 59, 73, 75, 111, 121, 169, 201, 209, 217
therapists, 9, 30, 32, 33, 111, 115
therapy, 31, 71, 108, 110
threatening e-mails, letters, journal entries, 95, 122
threats and acts of intimidation, 96, 122
time-shares, 23
torture of pets, 122
traffic records, 122
transcript of trial, 206
transcripts of depositions, 34, 73
transferring property, 192
TransUnion, 186
travel expenses for parenting time, 22
trial, 35, 45, 59, 75, 91, 114, 168, 172, 200–213
  benefits, 90
  risk factors, 83, 90
  steps in, 212
  testifying, 210
  witnesses, 209
trial briefs, 7
trial date, 6, 42, 45, 82, 201, 209
trial exhibits, 7, 207
trial judge, 46, 84, 90
trial notebook, 208
trial preparation, 192, 207,

About the Authors

Marlene A. Pontrelli is a member of Dickinson Wright, PLLC., and is co-chair of the family law practice group. She is also certified by the State Bar of Arizona as a specialist in family law; her practice focuses on all aspects of family law including dissolution of marriage, legal separation, post-dissolution modifications, paternity, and children's issues. She has been in practice for over thirty-two years. She is a judge *pro tem* for the Superior Court of Maricopa County in family law. Ms. Pontrelli is an adjunct faculty member at Arizona State University School of Law, where she teaches family law.

In 2005, she obtained her life coaching certificate through the Professional Coaching Institute. She has extensive trial and appellate experience including appearing before the Arizona Court of Appeals, Arizona Supreme Court, and Ninth Circuit Court of Appeals.

She has written several books including *Focus on Family Law* and *Daily Meditations for Healing from Divorce*. Ms. Pontrelli is a frequent lecturer in the area of family law. She has conducted numerous workshops and seminars throughout the country on parenting after divorce, time management, and balancing work and personal life.

Robert L. Schwartz has been practicing law in the state of Arizona for more than forty years. His courtroom skills were developed over the past forty-seven years. Starting as a prosecutor for the Maricopa County Attorney's Office wherein he tried numerous jury trials and progressing to practicing exclusively family law for the last thirty-five years.

An expert in the area of family law, Mr. Schwartz is a family law specialist certified by the State Bar of Arizona; he is a fellow in the American Academy of Matrimonial Lawyers and past president of the Arizona Chapter. He is also a founding member of the Arizona Family Law Institute, which consists of a two-day family law symposium held on an annual basis in the state of Arizona. He is a frequent lecturer in the area of family law and has been recognized as an expert in family law, both nationally and locally.

Mr. Schwartz has tried numerous family law cases involving the most complex and difficult of issues. He has handled many appeals, which have in some cases established family law within the state of Arizona or modified existing family law within the state.

Mr. Schwartz has been named by "Best Lawyers in America" for the practice of family law for more than twenty years. In addition, he has been named as Family Lawyer of the Year by Best Lawyer in America for 2010, 2018, 2020.

Divorce Titles from Addicus Books

Visit our online catalog at www.AddicusBooks.com

To Order Books:
Visit us online at: www.AddicusBooks.com
Call toll free: (800) 888-4741

Addicus Books
P. O. Box 45327
Omaha, NE 68145

Addicus Books is dedicated to publishing books
that comfort and educate.